Handbook of

Calisthenics

Hypertrophy and Free-Body Strength

*The Best Exercises, Workout Charts and Specific Nutrition
for Increasing Muscle Mass*

William Miller

Disclaimer

Summary

What does Calisthenics mean?

The term calisthenics comes from ancient Greek and is composed of two words: "kalos" means "beautiful" and "sthenos" means "strength." Literally translated, calisthenics therefore means "beautiful exercises to develop strength."

Calisthenics is a form of physical training that primarily uses one's own body weight to perform a wide range of exercises. It is a discipline that focuses on strength, endurance, flexibility, balance, and coordination without the use of additional equipment or weights. Calisthenic exercises include movements such as push-ups, pull-ups, lunges, planks, squats, and many others.

What makes calisthenics so unique is its versatility and adaptability to different fitness levels. Beginners can start with basic exercises such as knee push-ups or assisted lunges, while more experienced athletes can perform complex acrobatic exercises such as human flags or planks.

Calisthenics is based on a gradual progression: you start with simpler movements and progress to more complex movements as you gain strength and body control. This progressive approach prevents injury and builds a solid foundation of strength and endurance.

One of the most attractive aspects of calisthenics is that it can be practiced anywhere, without the need for expensive equipment or a gym. One can train outdoors, at home or in a park, using the surrounding elements such as bars, benches, or walls to perform the exercises. This freedom and flexibility make calisthenics very accessible to anyone who wants to train.

Calisthenics offers numerous health benefits. First, it develops muscle strength and tone throughout the body. Calisthenics exercises use several muscle groups simultaneously, improving functional strength and coordination. In addition, calisthenics promotes cardiorespiratory endurance, as many exercises are performed in high-intensity circuits. This type of training can improve the efficiency of the cardiovascular system and increase lung capacity.

In addition to strength and endurance, calisthenics also improves flexibility and balance. Many exercises require a wide range of joint movement and good body control in space. Regular practice of calisthenics can help increase muscle flexibility and improve balance and stability.

Another unique feature of calisthenics is the mind-body connection that develops through the exercise. Calisthenics exercises require one to be aware of one's condition and to focus on the correct execution of movements. This body awareness can also be transferred to other daily activities and improves posture, coordination, and body awareness.

The term "calisthenic" refers to a person who practices calisthenics. A calisthenic strives to develop physical strength and perform advanced movements using body weight training. One develops a good mind-body connection and a greater awareness of one's body and its capabilities.

In recent years, calisthenics has gained popularity around the world. Calisthenics competitions have become increasingly common events where athletes take part in competitions of strength, control, and creativity. In addition, online calisthenics communities provide support and inspiration to those who want to pursue this training path.

In summary, calisthenics is a form of physical training that uses body weight to develop strength, endurance, flexibility, balance, and coordination. It is a very versatile discipline that is suitable for people of all fitness levels, can be practiced anywhere, and offers numerous health benefits.

Frequently asked questions and myths to dispel about calisthenics.

Frequently asked questions about Calisthenics:

Is calisthenics suitable for everyone?
Calisthenics can be practiced by people of different ages and fitness levels. It can be adapted to individual abilities and can be intensified gradually over time.

Can I build muscle just by doing calisthenics?
Absolutely. Calisthenics uses your own body weight to develop endurance, strength, and muscle mass. Exercises such as pull-ups, push-ups, squats, and pistol squats can help build muscle and improve body composition.

Do I need a special facility or expensive equipment to practice Calisthenics?
Calisthenics is based on using your own body weight, so it does not require expensive equipment or special facilities. One can train in gyms, parks or even at home with dumbbells, parallel bars, and elastic bands. However, it is important to perform the exercises correctly to ensure the safety and effectiveness of the workout.

Can calisthenics help me lose weight?
Yes, calisthenics can help you lose weight by combining resistance exercises with high-intensity cardiovascular exercises. Calisthenics training burns calories, stimulates metabolism and promotes body fat loss.

False Myths about the Calisthenic Technique:

Calisthenics does not build muscle like dumbbell training.
This is a common myth. Calisthenics can be just as effective for muscle hypertrophy and strength development as weight training. Sequences and variations of Calisthenics exercises can be adapted to stimulate muscles appropriately.

Calisthenics is suitable only for experienced athletes.

Although some calisthenics exercises may seem advanced, calisthenics can be practiced at any fitness level. With the right progression and by learning proper execution techniques, even beginners can practice Calisthenics safely and effectively.

Calisthenics does not offer training variety.
Calisthenics offers a wide range of exercises and progressions that can be tailored to individual needs and goals. Strength, flexibility, balance, and body control exercises can be performed that provide a variety of stimulation and progressions over time.

Calisthenics does not take time.
Although calisthenics can be practiced anywhere and does not require expensive equipment, commitment and time are still needed to achieve significant results. Time and consistency in training are needed to improve strength, balance, and flexibility.

Thus, calisthenics is a sport suitable for people of different abilities, promotes muscle development, can be practiced anywhere without expensive equipment, and offers a variety of exercises. It is important to dispel common myths that may discourage people from practicing calisthenics. With commitment and the right progression, remarkable results can be achieved.

Calisthenics: where and how to start

If you want to start practicing calisthenics, you must first understand some basic concepts and follow a step-by-step approach to achieve safe and effective results. Here is a detailed guide on how to start practicing calisthenics.

Establish goals: Before you begin, clearly define your goals. You may want to increase your overall strength, improve endurance, increase flexibility, or achieve specific goals such as completing a pull-up at the barre. Clear goals will help you structure your training program and monitor your progress over time.

Fitness assessment: before beginning calisthenics, it is important to assess your current fitness level. Make sure you are in good health and have no injuries or illnesses that may require special attention. If in doubt, consult your doctor before starting a new exercise program.

Start with the basics: although calisthenics offers a wide range of complex movements, it is important to start with the basics. Basic movements include push-ups, lunges, planks, crunches, pull-ups, and squats. Take the time to properly master these movements before moving on to more advanced ones.

Learn proper technique: technique is critical in calisthenics. Practice movements in the correct form to avoid injury and maximize results. To learn proper techniques from the beginning, you can use video tutorials on the Internet or work with an experienced calisthenics coach.

Gradual increase: one of the keys to successful calisthenics is gradual increase. Do not try to perform advanced movements from the beginning but follow an exercise sequence that allows you to gradually build strength and endurance. For example, start with knee push-ups or assisted push-ups and then move on to traditional push-ups. This way you avoid overload and build a solid foundation.

Workout schedule: establish a regular workout schedule that includes exercises for the whole body. You can divide the workout into days, each dedicated to specific muscle groups, or do a full-body workout two or three times a week. Be sure to include upper and lower body, core, and flexibility exercises.

Rest and recovery: rest is important to allow the body to recover and adapt to training. Be sure to include rest days in your schedule and take time to recover. A good night's sleep, proper nutrition and hydration are also important for optimal recovery.

Monitor progress: track your progress over time. You can record the number of repetitions or sets you perform, the time you take to complete an exercise, or use other metrics to measure it. Monitoring progress motivates you and allows you to tailor your training to your results.

Expand your knowledge: Learn more and expand your knowledge of calisthenics. Explore new movements, study anatomy and proper exercise execution, follow talented calisthenics athletes and coaches on online platforms, and participate in communities of calisthenics enthusiasts to share experiences and inspire you.

Have fun: Calisthenics can be a fun and rewarding way to exercise. Experiment, try new movements, challenge yourself and have fun. The key to lasting commitment is finding joy in training and feeling motivated to achieve your goals.

Some of these basic concepts will be explained later.

Remember that calisthenics requires patience and consistency. Do not expect to achieve extraordinary results in a few days but be disciplined and consistent in your approach. With time and practice, you will notice significant improvements in strength, endurance, and overall physical performance.

Injury prevention in calisthenics and the importance of proper technique

Injury prevention is of paramount importance in calisthenics to ensure a safe and effective workout. One of the keys to injury prevention is proper exercise technique. When movements are performed correctly, excessive stress on joints is reduced and work is more efficient and balanced.

The importance of proper technique in calisthenics is obvious, as it maximizes the benefits of training and minimizes the risk of injury. Below are some important points to keep in mind to avoid injury during calisthenics training:

Learn proper technique: before beginning more advanced exercises, basic techniques must be mastered. These include correct posture, body alignment, use of the right muscles, and proper breathing. If necessary, seek help from a coach or watch reliable tutorials to learn the right techniques.

Gradual increase: do not try to do advanced exercises from the beginning. Start with simple movements and gradually progress to more complex and intense exercises. Gradual increases allow the body to adapt and reduce the risk of overexertion or injury.

Warm up properly: Take time to warm up before beginning physical activity. This includes activities such as light jogging, jumping in place, joint rotations, and dynamic stretching movements. Warming up increases body temperature, improves blood circulation and prepares muscles, tendons, and joints for exercise.

Listen to your body: pay attention to your body's signals when you exercise. If you feel pain or strange sensations during an exercise, stop immediately and assess the situation. Do not overload your body and respect the recovery time your body needs to regenerate.

Balance between strength and flexibility: in calisthenics it is important to develop both strength and flexibility. A strong but inflexible muscle can be prone to strain and injury. Be sure to incorporate stretching exercises into your routine and work on the balance between strength and flexibility.

Use proper equipment: when performing calisthenics exercises, be sure to use proper and safe equipment. Make sure the bars, supports or resistance bands are sturdy and in good condition. Use cushions or mats to soften falls or impacts.

Recovery and rest: do not underestimate the importance of recovery and rest in the injury prevention process. Allow yourself time to rest and recover after intense training. Quality sleep, healthy eating, and recovery techniques such as massage or muscle relaxation can help reduce the risk of injury.

Always remember that safety comes first when exercising. Do not hesitate to consult a fitness expert or doctor if you have any concerns or health problems. Calisthenics offers many benefits, but for best results, mindful, responsible, and safe exercise is important.

The adaptability of calisthenics to different age groups and fitness levels

The adaptability of calisthenics to different age groups and fitness levels is one of the great advantages of this form of training. Calisthenics can be practiced by people of all ages and fitness levels and offers a wide range of benefits to both beginners and experienced athletes.

Beginners: calisthenics is particularly suitable for beginners, as it provides a solid foundation for developing strength, flexibility, and body control. Basic exercises such as push-ups, lunges and squats can be easily adapted to individual physical abilities. You can start with simplified variations of the exercises, reduce the intensity, or use auxiliary tools such as elastic bands or parallel bars to make them easier to perform.

Advanced: As you gain strength and body control, you can move on to more complex calisthenics exercises. Pull-ups, muscle-ups, human flags, and handstand push-ups are just a few of the exercises that can challenge higher-level athletes. It is important to continue to work on proper technique and increase strength to improve performance.

Advanced: Experienced athletes can push their limits in calisthenics by experimenting with advanced movements such as front raises, planking, back raises, and one-handed push-ups. These exercises require a high level of strength, flexibility and body control and can be an exciting challenge for even the most experienced athletes. It is important to proceed gradually and work systematically to avoid injury.

Seniors: calisthenics can also be adapted to the needs of the elderly. Free-body exercises such as walking, lunges, squats, and balance exercises can improve muscle strength, endurance, mobility, and balance in the elderly. It is important to work with a fitness professional who has experience in adapting exercise for the elderly, considering physical limitations and overall health.

Regardless of age or fitness level, calisthenics offers a number of benefits for the body and mind. The main benefits are increasing muscle strength and endurance, improving flexibility, correcting posture, increasing metabolism, and preventing cardiovascular health. In addition, calisthenics works several muscle groups simultaneously, stimulating the body in a functional and comprehensive way.

In summary, calisthenics is suitable for different ages and fitness levels and offers a variety of exercises and progressions that can be tailored to individual needs. Whether you are a beginner, intermediate or senior, calisthenics is a versatile and effective option for improving strength, flexibility, and overall fitness.

Calisthenics Exercises for Beginners

Before starting any workout, it is essential to warm up the body properly to prepare it for physical exertion without risking physically unpleasant scenarios.
Let's look together at the importance of warm-up and cool-down in calisthenics.

The importance of these two factors is critical for preparing the body for training and for proper recovery after training. Both elements are important for ensuring optimal performance, preventing injury, and promoting good overall health.

Warm-up is a preliminary phase of training in which body temperature is gradually increased and muscles, tendons and joints are activated. This phase is important because it adequately prepares the body for the physical activity that will follow. Here are some reasons why warm-up is crucial in calisthenics:

Increased body temperature: warming increases body temperature, in turn promoting better blood circulation. In this way, muscles are warmed up and better prepared for physical activities.

Improved flexibility: during warm-up, muscles, tendons, and joints become more elastic and flexible. This allows exercises to be performed with a full range of motion and reduces the risk of injury due to limited joint mobility.

Activating the cardiovascular system: during the warm-up phase, the heart starts pumping blood faster to supply the muscles with oxygen and nutrients. This prepares the cardiovascular system for the intense physical activity that will follow during calisthenics.

Nervous system activation: warming up also stimulates the nervous system and improves the connection between the brain and muscles. This improves coordination and movement control during exercise.

Cooldown is the final phase of training in which we gradually return to a state of rest. This phase is just as important as the warm-up and serves to relax the muscles, reduce lactic acid buildup, and ensure proper recovery after the workout. This is why cooling down is so important in calisthenics:

Lactic acid reduction: during intense exercise, lactic acid builds up in muscles and can cause muscle fatigue and stiffness. Cooling helps reduce lactic acid buildup and accelerates muscle recovery.

Restoration of heart and respiratory rate: during fatigue, the heart and lungs gradually return to their resting rhythm. This allows the body to recover and return to cardiorespiratory balance.

Prevention of dizziness or fainting: Defibrillation helps prevent abrupt changes in blood pressure and reduces the risk of dizziness or fainting that can occur after strenuous exercise.

Promotes muscle recovery: cooling down facilitates blood flow to muscles and provides them with the nutrients they need to repair and grow. This promotes faster recovery and positive adaptation to training stimuli.

In summary, warm-up and cool-down are crucial aspects of calisthenics. Both play a key role in preparing the body for training, improving performance, and preventing injury. Devoting adequate time to these phases before and after training can make all the difference in maximizing the benefits of calisthenics and ensuring a safe and effective workout.

Now that we know how to do this, let's look together at some exercises for beginners.

Beginners to calisthenics have the opportunity to learn a wide range of exercises that are accessible and appropriate for their fitness level. Starting with exercises that match one's limits and abilities is critical to building a solid foundation and gradually developing strength and body control. The following pages illustrate a list of exercises for beginners in calisthenics:

Push-ups with support on the knees: push-ups are a basic exercise in gymnastics. For beginners, you can reduce the intensity and make it easier to perform if you lean on your knees instead of your toes. Be sure to keep your body straight and lower yourself slowly and in a controlled manner.

Find out here how to correctly perform push-ups with support on the knees:

Get on all fours on the floor with your knees and hands resting on the floor. Make sure your hands are slightly wider than your shoulders and your knees are in line with your hips.
Move your feet slightly away from your body so that your weight is evenly distributed between your knees and hands, this is the starting position.
Keeping your body straight, bend your elbows and slowly lower your chest toward the floor. Try to maintain control of the movement, avoiding lowering the chest or lifting the buttocks.
Keep going down until your chest is just above the floor or until you reach the point where you still feel comfortable. Make sure you have good posture, with your abdominal muscles slightly tight and your neck in line with your spine.

Once you reach the lowest point, push with your hands, and return to the starting position, fully extending your arms.
Repeat the movement for the desired number of repetitions.
When performing knee push-ups, it is important to focus on proper technique and maintain full control of the movement. Be sure to breathe regularly during the exercise, inhaling when you lower and exhaling when you raise. As you gain strength and confidence, you can gradually begin to perform traditional push-ups on your toes and work toward perfect form. With regular, progressive training, you can improve the strength and endurance of the muscles involved in push-ups.

Assisted lunges: lunges are ideal for training leg and gluteal muscles. To simplify execution, you can use a support such as a chair or bench to maintain balance during the lunge. As you gain strength, you can gradually give up the support and switch to traditional lunges.

Find out how to perform assisted lunges correctly here:

Place your feet shoulder-width apart, pay attention to an upright posture and look straight ahead.
Look for a stable support, such as a chair or bench. Place it in front of you and put your right foot on the base, your left foot stays on the ground, your heel is raised.

Shift your weight to your left foot, bend your right knee and lower your body toward the floor. Try to keep your torso straight and your left knee in line with your ankle.
Drop lower until your right knee forms a 90-degree angle. Make sure you maintain control of the movement and do not tilt your upper body forward.
Stop for a moment in the lowest position, then push back with the right foot and return to the starting position, fully extending the leg.
Repeat the movement for the desired number of repetitions, then switch to the other leg.
Try to maintain a regular rhythm and good posture while performing supported lunges. Focus on activating the leg muscles and maintaining balance throughout the movement.

By increasing strength and flexibility, you can gradually reduce support or perform traditional lunges without support. The goal is to gradually improve leg strength and stability so that you can perform lunges without assistance.

Remember to always listen to your body and pay attention to tension or pain during your workout. If you have stability problems or other physical limitations, consult a fitness professional or physical therapist individually.

Plank: this is an effective exercise to strengthen the center of the body and improve balance. First lie on your stomach on the floor, then raise your body while bending your arms at a 90-degree angle and keeping your legs extended. Hold this position as long as possible and be sure to form a straight line from head to toe.

Find out how to perform the plank correctly here:

Lie face down on the floor. Place your forearms on the floor so that they are parallel to each other, with your elbows directly under your shoulders. Your arms should be at a 90-degree angle.
Lift your body by leaning on your forearms and toes. Make sure your body forms a straight line from head to toe and avoid dropping your hips or lifting your pelvis too much.
Contract your abdominal and gluteal muscles to maintain a stable position. Try to keep your trunk muscles active and breathe regularly during the exercise.
Hold the plank for the desired duration. If you are a beginner, you can start with 20-30 seconds and then gradually increase the duration if you have more strength and endurance.
When you are ready to finish the exercise, slowly lower your body to the floor and return to the starting position.

When performing the plank, it is important to maintain good posture and control breathing. Avoid raising or lowering your hips or bending your back. The goal is to maintain a straight, stable line during the exercise.

As your trunk strength increases, you can increase the intensity of the exercise by performing variations such as the side plank, lifting a leg or arm, or placing your feet on a ball to make stability more difficult.
The plank can be performed as part of a longer workout routine or as a warm-up exercise before other exercises. It is a great way to strengthen the core and improve posture and stability of the whole body.

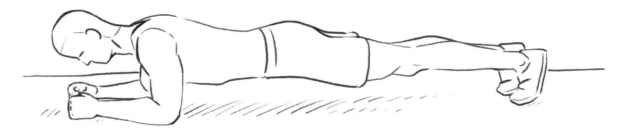

Supported pull-ups: pull-ups on the bar are a great exercise to develop upper body strength, particularly the shoulder and arm muscles. For beginners, supported pull-ups are a good option to get started. You can use a rubber band or footrest to make it easier to lift during the exercise. If you gain strength, you can reduce the support and switch to unsupported pull-ups.

Find out how to properly perform supported pull-ups here:

Find a pull-up bar and an aid such as a rubber band or leg support. Make sure the bar is so high that you can fully extend your arms when standing.

Arrange your hands slightly more shoulder-width apart at the bar, palms facing you. Grasp the rod as you stand on your tiptoes or place your knees on the support platform.

Start with your arms fully extended, maintain an upright posture and look upward, this is your starting position.

Maintaining control of the movement, bend your arms and pull your body upward toward the bar. Focus on activating the back and shoulder muscles during the movement.

Keep going up until your chin reaches the same height as the pole or until you reach the last point where you still feel comfortable. Be sure to maintain control of the movement and avoid swinging or lifting your legs for support.

Stop for a moment in the highest position and then controlling the movement by extending your arms to return to the starting position.

Repeat the movement as many times as you like.

During assisted pull-ups, it is important to have good posture and move in a controlled manner. Be sure to breathe regularly during the exercise, inhaling when you pull up and exhaling when you extend your arms.

As you gain strength and confidence, you can gradually reduce the device or elastic band support and work to perform traditional pull-ups without assistance.

Remember to adapt the exercise to your individual abilities and limitations. With time and consistent practice, you will be able to perform full pull-ups and experience the benefits of Calisthenics for strength and muscle building.

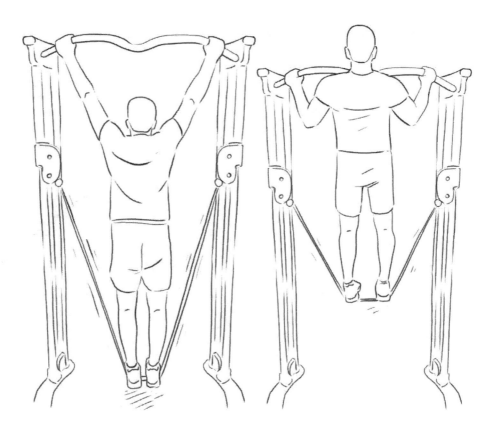

Assisted squats: squats are a key movement for training leg and gluteal muscles. To simplify execution, you can perform assisted squats by holding on to a chair or bar to maintain balance. Be sure to maintain good form and that your knees stay in line with your toes during the movement.

Find out how to perform assisted squats correctly here:

Stand upright with your feet shoulder-width apart. Use a stable support such as a chair or bench and lean on it with your hands to keep your balance.

Assume an upright posture, with your chest lifted and your gaze upward.
Start by lowering your body, bending your knees, and pushing your hips back as if you were sitting in a chair. Try to keep your weight on your heels throughout the movement.
Keep going down until your thighs are parallel to the floor or until you reach the point where you feel comfortable. Be sure to keep your back straight and do not tilt your upper body forward.
Stay in the lowest position for a moment, then push back your heels and return to the starting position, fully extending your legs.
Repeat the movement for the desired number of repetitions.
When performing assisted squats, it is important to focus on proper technique and move in a controlled manner. Be sure to breathe regularly during the exercise by exhaling as you lower and lift.

As you increase your strength and confidence, you can gradually reduce the support and work to perform conventional squats without assistance. You can also increase the intensity of the exercise by holding weights or using a lower chair or bench.

Remember to always listen to your body and pay attention to tension or pain during your workout. If you have stability problems or other physical limitations, consult a fitness professional or physical therapist individually.

With time and consistent practice, assisted squats will help you develop strength and stability in your legs, thus improving your endurance and your ability to perform more advanced movements in calisthenics technique.

Sit-ups: these are a classic exercise to strengthen abdominal muscles. Lie on your back, bend your knees, place the soles of your feet on the floor and put your hands behind your head. Lift your head and shoulders off the floor, tense your abs, and then slowly lower. Do not pull your head with your hands to avoid neck tension.

Find out how to perform sit-ups correctly here:

First, lie on a mat or soft surface with your back. Bend your knees so that your feet are flat on the floor and place your feet parallel and shoulder-width apart. Arms can be crossed behind the head, in front of the chest or resting on the side, depending on personal preference.

Tighten your abdominal muscles, bring your chin to your chest, and lift your head, shoulders, and upper body slightly off the floor. Try to focus on the rectus abdominis and avoid pulling the neck or using momentum.

Stop for a moment in the highest position and focus on activating the abdominals. Pay attention to good straight abdominal muscle tension and avoid bending your back or lifting your legs during the movement.

Controllably lower the upper body to the starting position, with the lower back lightly touching the floor without fully relaxing the abdominal muscles.

Repeat the movement with the desired number of repetitions.

When performing so-called sit-ups, it is important to have correct posture and control the movement. Avoid lifting the neck or pulling the head with your hands, as this can stiffen the neck and reduce the effectiveness of the exercise. Instead, focus on contracting the abdominal muscles and lifting the upper body using only abdominal strength.

Remember to breathe regularly during the exercise by exhaling when you raise your upper body and inhaling when you lower your upper body. If you want to increase the intensity of the exercise, you can try variations such as oblique crunches or inverted crunches that involve more abdominal muscles.

As with all exercises, you should listen to your body and pay attention to any tension or pain. If you have back or shoulder problems, consult a fitness professional or physical therapist.

Sit-ups are a great addition to your exercise routine to strengthen and define your abdominal muscles. With time and consistent practice, you will be able to perform all types of exercises with greater ease and your core will become strong and stable.

Superman: Superman is an exercise that strengthens the lower back and back muscles. Lie on your stomach and stretch your arms out in front of you. At the same time, lift your arms, legs and chest off the floor and hold this position for a few seconds before releasing it again. During the exercise, focus on the correct contraction of your back muscles.

Find out how to correctly perform the Superman exercise here:

First, lie on a mat or soft base with your stomach. Your legs should be extended, and your arms stretched forward, parallel to the floor.
Contract your back and gluteal muscles as you begin to lift your arms, head, and legs off the floor at the same time. Imagine yourself flying like Superman.
Hold the raised position for a few seconds, trying to keep the body in a straight line. Focus on activating the back and gluteal muscles.
Return in a controlled manner to the starting position and lower arms, head, and legs.
Repeat the movement again.
In doing so, avoid stretching the back or lifting the shoulders during the movement. Focus on the back and buttocks to lift the body without overstretching the neck.

Remember to breathe regularly during the exercise, inhaling when you lift your body and exhaling when you return to the starting position.

You can adapt the Superman exercise to your needs and abilities. If you are a beginner, you can start with a few repetitions and gradually increase the number as you gain more strength and endurance. You can also try variations such as the modified Superman, in which you lift only your upper or lower limbs, one at a time.
The Superman exercise is a good addition to your exercise program to strengthen your back and improve your posture. Please note that if you have back or shoulder problems, you should consult a fitness professional or physical therapist before you experience much pain.

Mountain climbers: this is a cardiovascular exercise that involves the whole body. Take the plank position, then alternately pull the right and left knee toward the chest in a quick movement. Keep an even pace during the exercise and try to activate the abdominal and leg muscles.

Here find out how to properly execute the mountain climbers:

Start in a high plank position, with your hands resting on the floor at shoulder width and your arms fully extended. Keep your body in a straight line, with your legs extended behind you and your feet perpendicular on your toes.
Contract your abs and lift one knee toward your chest, bringing your foot as close to your hands as possible. Keep the rest of the body stable and upright during the movement.
Stretch the raised leg in a controlled manner in the plank position, bringing the other knee to the chest at the same time. Alternate your leg movements quickly and continuously, as if you were "climbing" a mountain.
Keep a steady, controlled pace during exercise and pay attention to good posture and body alignment.

Perform the exercise for a certain amount of time or for a desired number of repetitions.
When performing mountain climbers, it is important to apply good technique and control the movement. Avoid lifting the pelvis too much or bending the back during the movement. Focus on activating the abdominal muscles and arms to guide the movement of the legs.
Remember to breathe regularly during exercise and maintain a steady breathing rhythm. Breathing in and out regularly during exercise will help you maintain good oxygenation and improve your endurance.
You can adapt the climber to your needs and abilities. If you are a beginner, you can start with a slower pace and gradually increase the intensity and speed if you have more stamina. You can also perform variations, such as the alternating climber.

Mountain climbers is a great addition to a calisthenics training program because it targets different parts of the body and provides a full body workout. Be sure to listen to your body and pay attention to any tension or pain during exercise. If you have shoulder or wrist problems, you can try variations or get individual advice from a fitness expert.

Russian Twist: This exercise focuses on strengthening the oblique muscles. Sit on the floor, lift your legs off the floor and tilt them at a 90-degree angle. Rotate your upper body from side to side, touching the floor with your hands with each extension. Be sure to tighten your abdominal muscles and maintain good posture during the exercise.

Find out how to perform Russian twists correctly here:

First, sit on the floor with your knees bent, with your feet resting on the floor. Tilt your upper body back slightly, leaving your back straight and forming an angle of about 45 degrees with the ground.

Cross your hands in front of your chest, cross your arms or grab a heavy weight or object to increase the intensity of the exercise.
Contract the abdominal muscles and rotate the upper body to the right, bringing the hands or object to the right side of the body. Maintain abdominal contraction and control of the movement.
Return to the middle position and rotate the upper body to the left, bringing the hands or object to the left side of the body.
Continue alternating left and right rotations in a smooth and controlled manner.
When performing Russian rotations, it is important to have good posture and move in a controlled manner. Avoid tilting your torso too far back or lifting your feet off the floor during the rotation. Focus on activating the oblique abdominals and trunk control during rotations.

Remember to breathe regularly during the exercise, inhale into the middle position and exhale during rotations. Keep a regular, controlled rhythm and avoid sudden or rapid movements that could interfere with technique.

You can customize the Russian rotations according to your needs and abilities. If you are a beginner, you can start with smaller movements and gradually increase the amplitude of the rotations if you gain more strength and flexibility. You can also increase the intensity of the exercise by using a weight or heavy object while performing the rotations.
Russian rotations are a great addition to a calisthenics training program because they incorporate the trunk muscles into a rotational movement. Remember to listen to your body and pay attention to any tension or pain during the exercise. If you have back or neck problems, you can try variations or get individual advice from a fitness professional.

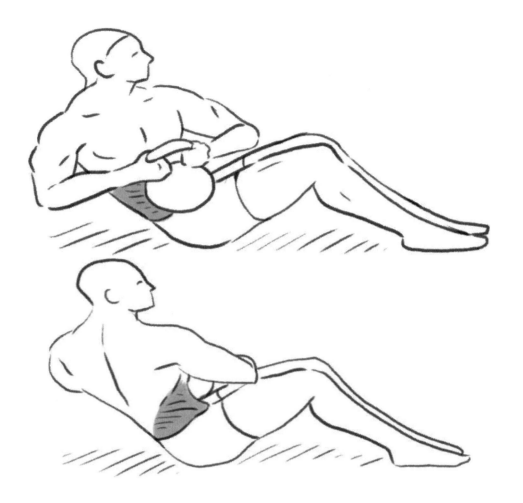

Stretching: Don't forget to stretch after every workout. Stretching exercises will help you improve the flexibility of your muscles and prevent injuries. Focus on areas such as legs, arms, back, and neck and hold the positions for at least 20 to 30 seconds.

Here are some common stretching exercises from calisthenics:

Calf lengthening
First, stand in front of a wall, with one foot slightly behind the other. Bend your front knee and extend the heel of your back foot toward the floor. Hold the position for about 30 seconds, then switch legs.

Quadriceps stretch: lie on the right side, bend the left knee, and grab the ankle with the left hand. Pull the foot toward the buttocks, keeping the upper body straight, hold the position for about 30 seconds, then switch sides.
Sciatic muscle stretch: sit on the floor, extend one leg forward and angle the other, with the foot resting on the inside of the opposite thigh. Bend your upper body forward and reach for the foot of your outstretched leg. Hold this position for about 30 seconds, then switch legs.

23

Hip flexor stretching

Get into a lunge position, with one knee bent at 90 degrees and the other extended behind you. Bring your upper body forward with your back straight until you feel a slight tension in your front hip. Hold this position for about 30 seconds, then switch legs.

Lengthening of pectoral muscles

Stand in front of a wall and extend your right arm at shoulder height along the wall, with your palm resting on the wall. Rotate your torso to the left with your arm extended until you feel a slight tension in your chest and shoulder. Hold the position for about 30 seconds, then switch sides.

.

During stretching, it is important to breathe regularly and relax the muscles to be stretched. Avoid forcing the movements too much and try to get a pleasant stretching sensation without severe pain. Remember that warming up before stretching can improve the elasticity of the muscles.

It is recommended that the stretching program is performed after the workout or at a different time than the main workout. This warms the muscles and prepares them for stretching.

Remember that each person has his or her own degree of joint flexibility and mobility. Therefore, it is important to tailor stretching exercises to your abilities and limitations. If you have any health problems or injuries, consult a fitness professional or physical therapist for personalized advice on stretching and calisthenics best practices.

Don't forget to warm up properly before exercises and always listen to your body. Do not overdo the intensity or duration of your workout and allow yourself time to rest and recover between sessions. Through consistent practice and gradual progress, you will achieve more complex and challenging exercises in Calisthenics.

What Calisthenics equipment can you train with at home? What about at the gym?

Calisthenics is a type of workout based on the use of one's own body weight to develop strength, endurance, and flexibility. Calisthenics is a very versatile workout in that it can be performed either at home or in a gym with minimal or special equipment. Let's take a look at equipment options for Calisthenics in both environments.

Calisthenics workout at home:

Pull-up bar: The pull-up bar is an indispensable tool for training many exercises in gymnastics, such as assisted pull-ups and lunges. There are different types of pull-up bars, such as bars that can be attached to the door frame or freestanding bars.

Parallel bars: these are small parallel bars that can be used for exercises such as push-ups, Dips and L-seat exercises. They can be used to develop upper limb and trunk strength.

Backboard: a backboard is an alternative to a pull-up bar that can be attached to the door frame. It provides greater stability and strength, allowing for a variety of supported pull-ups and lunges.

Padded mat: A padded mat is useful for performing floor exercises such as sit-ups, lunges, and abdominal exercises.

Exercise ball: an exercise ball can be used for stability and balance exercises, such as lunges on the ball or push-ups with hands on the ball.

Calisthenics Workout at the Gym :

Pull-up bar: even at the gym, the pull-up bar is an indispensable device for calisthenics. The gym can offer different options of pull-up bars, such as fixed bars or extendable bars, which can be adjusted to different heights.

Dip Bar: With Dip bars, you can perform exercises such as Dips and L-Sits safely and effectively. They are designed to support your body weight and offer different grip and height options.

TRX or stretch bands: stretch bands or the TRX system can be used for a wide range of exercises in calisthenics. They offer adjustable resistance and support for exercises such as push-ups, assisted pull-ups, and supported lunges.

Bench or multi-position bench: a bench can be useful for exercises such as sit-ups, push-ups, and Russian rotations. A multi-position bench offers the ability to perform exercises at different inclinations, making the workout more varied and challenging.

Platform or jumping level: a jumping platform or trampoline can be used for plyometric exercises and to improve leg strength, such as jumping or lunges.

Importantly, Calisthenics focuses on the use of body weight and the proper execution of exercises. Therefore, even without special equipment, it is possible to train effectively with your body alone. At home or at the gym, it is important to have the right technique, a balance between strength and agility, and a gradual increase in training intensity.

How to build a basic Calisthenics program

Structuring a Calisthenics training program requires careful planning to achieve maximum results and avoid injury. The following steps should help you to create a basic Calisthenics training plan.

First, set the goals you want to achieve with your workout. You may want to increase your strength, define your muscles, improve your endurance, or work on certain skills such as pull-ups or L sits.

Next, decide how many times a week you want to train with Calisthenics. Take into consideration your current fitness level, the time available, and your body's ability to recover. Start with a weekly frequency that allows you to gradually get used to training, such as two to three sessions per week.

Choose a set of basic calisthenics exercises that include all major muscle groups. Be sure to choose exercises that match your current fitness level and correspond to your goals. Basic exercises can include pull-ups, push-ups, lunges, planks, sit-ups, and many other variations.

Organize your workout into units that focus on specific muscle groups or goals. For example, you might devote one unit to pull-ups and push-ups, another to lunges and leg exercises, and another to abdominal muscles and core stability exercises. This way you can train each area in a targeted way and ensure the right recovery time for your muscles.

Determine the number of sets and repetitions for each exercise. As a beginner, start with two or three sets of eight to 12 repetitions for each exercise. Over time, you can increase the number of sets or repetitions or introduce more advanced variations of the exercises.

Don't forget to include rest days in your Calisthenics program; recovery is important to allow your muscles to recover and grow. You can plan active rest days during which you perform mobility exercises, stretching or light activities such as swimming or yoga.

In Calisthenics, gradual increase is key. As you get stronger and master the movements better, you can increase the intensity of your workout by introducing more challenging variations of exercises or adding new exercises to your form.

Variety is the key to avoiding boredom and stimulating your muscles in different ways. Add new exercises, try advanced variations, or change the order of exercises to challenge your body and make steady progress.

Track your progress in Calisthenics training. Track your performance and body weight to assess your progress over time and make any changes to your training program.

If you are new to calisthenics or have special goals, it may be helpful to contact a qualified coach or personal trainer who specializes in calisthenics. He or she can help you create a personalized program, guide you in the proper execution of exercises, and assist you in training.

Remember to tailor the exercise program to your needs and goals. Experiment, listen to your body, and modify the program accordingly to get the best results through exercise.

Practical Example of a Weekly Training Split

Day 1:

3 sets of push-ups (8-12 repetitions)
3 sets of supported pull-ups (8-12 repetitions)
3 sets of lunges (8-12 repetitions per leg)
3 sets of Planks (30-60 seconds)
3 sets of sit-ups (12-15 repetitions)

Day 2:

3 sets of supported squats (8-12 repetitions)
3 sets of push-ups balancing on the knees (8-12 repetitions)
3 sets of supported lunges (8-12 repetitions per leg)
3 sets of supported pull-ups with elastic band (8-12 repetitions)
3 sets of Russian Twist (12-15 repetitions per part)

Day 3:

3 Lateral Planks (30-60 seconds)
3 sets of lunges (8-12 repetitions per leg)
3 sets of sit-ups (12-15 repetitions)
3 sets of supported pull-ups (8-12 repetitions)
3 sets of alpinists (12-15 repetitions per leg)

This is just one example of how a basic training program could be constructed. You can adapt it to your preferences, goals, and fitness level. Always remember to start with a warm-up workout before each training session and allow time for active rest between sessions. Also, remember to gradually make it more challenging over time by increasing the number of repetitions, the difficulty level of the exercises, or the intensity of the workout to continue to challenge your body and make progress.

Pulling, pushing and abdominal exercises

Traction exercises

Pulling exercises are an essential part of calisthenics and are ideal for developing upper body strength, particularly the back and arm muscles. For Calisthenics beginners, there are several pulling exercises you can include in your training program to build the strength you need.

Rubber band assisted pull-ups: with this exercise you can start gradually and slowly develop the strength needed for full pull-ups. Attach a strong rubber band to a frame above you and grasp it with your hands at shoulder width. Make sure the band is taut, then bend your knees or place your feet on a platform to support them. Pull the band upward until your chin is over the bar, paying attention to good posture and tension in your back muscles. Slowly return to the starting position, moving in a controlled manner.

Supported pull-ups with a chair or step: this exercise is similar to supported pull-ups with a rubber band, but instead of a rubber band use a chair or stepper. Place a chair or stepper under the pull-up bar. Grasp the bar with your hands shoulder-width apart and place your feet on the chair or stepper. Pull yourself up until your chin is over the bar, paying attention to good posture and tension in your back muscles. Slowly return to the starting position.

Negative pull-ups: Negative pull-ups are an excellent exercise for building strength in the eccentric phase of the pull-up movement. First, jump upward to reach the starting position with your chin over the bar, then slowly begin the downward movement while controlling the movement until your arms are fully extended. You can use a footrest to get on the bar or get help from a step or a friend/partner.

Australian pull-ups: this exercise is an excellent alternative for developing the strength needed for full pull-ups. Stand under a bar or Smith machine at a height where you can grab the bar at shoulder width. Keep your body straight and tighten your back muscles as you pull upward until your chest or chin reaches the bar. Slowly return to the starting position.

Australian pull-ups with raised feet: this variation of the Australian pull-up allows you to increase the intensity of the exercise. Stand under a bar or Smith Machine bar and grab it with a handle at shoulder width. Lift your feet onto a stand so that your body forms a straight line.
Pull upward until your chest or chin reaches the bar, then slowly return to the starting position.

Remember that proper execution of exercises is critical to avoid injury and maximize results. Maintain good posture, tighten back muscles and control movement during pull-ups. Start with a number of sets and repetitions that will allow you to perform the exercises correctly and gradually. As you get stronger and master the exercise better, you can increase the intensity and the number of sets and repetitions.

Pushing exercises

Flexion (push) exercises within calisthenics focus on developing strength in the upper body, particularly in the shoulder, chest, and triceps areas. Here are some flexion exercises suitable for Calisthenics beginners:

Knee push-ups: knee push-ups are a variation of classic push-ups, where you can reduce the intensity of the exercise. Stand on all fours, with your knees on the floor and your hands slightly further apart than shoulder-width apart. Bend your arms and lower your body toward the floor, keeping your body straight. Then push your body upward until your arms are fully extended. Repeat the movement in the desired number of repetitions.

Incline push-ups: incline push-ups are a lighter alternative to conventional push-ups. Find an elevated area, such as a bench or step. Place your hands slightly wider than shoulder-width on the raised surface and extend your legs behind you, keeping your body straight. Bend your arms and lower your body toward the raised area, maintaining a stable posture. Then push your body upward until your arms are fully extended. Repeat the movement in the desired number of repetitions.

Chair push-ups: this exercise is a useful option for all beginners. Place your hands slightly wider than shoulder-width on a chair or a stable, raised surface. Extend your legs behind you and keep your body straight. Bend your arms and lower your body toward the floor, pushing your chest toward the chair. Then push your body upward until your arms are fully extended. Repeat the movement in the desired number of repetitions.

Chair Dips: these are an effective exercise to strengthen the triceps. Rest your hands on the edge of a stable chair, with your legs stretched out in front of you and your heels resting on the floor. Bend your arms and lower your body toward the floor, keeping your body straight. Then push your body upward until your arms are fully extended. Repeat the movement for the desired number of repetitions.

Rubber band shoulders: this exercise is ideal for training shoulder strength. Attach a strong rubber band to a stable structure above you. Grasp the end of the rubber band with your hands positioned slightly farther than shoulder width apart. Raise your arms upward and fully extend your arms above your head. Slowly return to the starting position and control the movement. Repeat the movement for the desired number of repetitions.

Remember to perform the exercises correctly, assume good posture and control the movement. Start with a number of sets and repetitions that will allow you to perform the exercises correctly and gradually. As you get stronger and master the exercises better, you can increase the intensity and the number of sets and repetitions.

Exercises for the abdomen

Abdominal muscle training is an essential element of calisthenics to create a solid foundation for core strength. Here are some abdominal exercises you can include in your Calisthenics program:

Sit-Up: The sit-up or crunch is a classic abdominal exercise. Lie on your back, bend your knees, and place your feet on the floor. Cross your hands behind your head or in front of your chest. Lift your head and shoulders off the floor and squeeze your abs without lifting your back completely off the floor. Release slowly and repeat the movement for the desired number of repetitions.

Leg Lift: This exercise mainly trains the lower abdominal muscles, lying on your back and stretching your legs. Slowly lift the legs upward, keeping the legs straight and the abdominal muscles taut. Stop when the legs are perpendicular to the floor, then slowly lower the legs back to the starting position. You can also perform this exercise with bent knees if you have difficulty keeping your legs straight.

Plank: Plank is a basic exercise to strengthen the abdominal and core muscles. Lie face down on the floor and rest on your elbows and toes. Keep your body straight and lifted off the floor, tighten your abdominal muscles and hold the position for a certain amount of time, such as 30 to 60 seconds.

Side plank: side plank is a variation in which the oblique muscles are also stressed. Stand on one side and place one elbow and the side of one foot on the floor. Lift your body in a straight line, tense your abs and hold the position for a period of time. Repeat the exercise on the other side.

Russian Twists: This exercise stresses the oblique abdominals. Sit on the floor with knees bent and feet planted on the floor. Tilt your upper body slightly, keeping your back straight. Grab a weight or medicine ball with both hands and rotate your upper body from side to side, with the weight touching the floor on each side.

Be sure to perform the exercises with proper technique and focus on tensing the abdominal muscles with each movement. Start with a number of sets and repetitions that will allow you to perform the exercises correctly and gradually. As you get stronger and master the exercises better, you can increase the intensity and the number of sets and repetitions.

The connection between mind and body and the importance of body perception

The connection between mind and body is a crucial aspect of Calisthenics training that goes beyond simply performing physical exercises. It involves the ability to regulate thoughts and to concentrate. This deep connection between mind and body is critical to getting the most out of your calisthenics training and achieving your goals.
Body awareness in Calisthenics is the ability to perceive and understand the body's movements, sensations, and reactions during training. This includes awareness of posture, alignment, breathing and muscle tension. If you are aware of your body, you can perform exercises more accurately, fluidly, and efficiently, thus maximizing the benefits of your workout.

A key element in the connection between the body and the mind in Calisthenics is concentration. During training, it is important to focus completely on the execution of the exercises and hide external distractions. Concentration allows you to direct the flow of thoughts and focus on the feeling of muscle contraction and stretching, correct body alignment, and correct breathing. In this way you can improve the precision and quality of your movements.

The importance of the connection between body and mind goes beyond just performing the exercises. If you are aware of your body during training, you can achieve better coordination and control of movement. Also, with the help of body perception, you can detect signs of fatigue or tension and adjust your training accordingly to prevent injury and optimize results.

The practice of body awareness in Calisthenics can be developed through various strategies, some useful suggestions are:

1. Practice meditation or relaxation before training to calm the mind and focus attention on the body.
2. Perform dynamic stretching exercises to improve mobility and awareness of different muscle groups.
3. Perform breathing control exercises to learn, consciously breathe and adapt to your body's needs during exercise. With stabilization and balance exercises you will develop greater awareness of body alignment and postural control.
4. Take the time to observe and analyze your movements during training and note any postural errors, limitations, or technical mistakes. Experiment with visual feedback such as videos to observe and correct your technique.
5. Working on the connection between body and mind requires practice and consistency. The more you practice mindfulness, the more you will improve your connection and performance. Body awareness not only improves physical results, but also contributes to overall well-being, stress management, and the promotion of a balanced state of mind during training.

Pros and cons of Calisthenics

Calisthenics, training with one's own body weight has become increasingly popular in recent years because it is practical and offers a complete workout. Like any type of workout, calisthenics has advantages and disadvantages. Let's look at these in detail.

Benefits of Calisthenics

- Accessibility: calisthenics does not require expensive or complex equipment. You can work out anywhere, even at home or in a park, using only your own body weight. This makes calisthenics an accessible option for everyone, with no restrictions in terms of access to a gym or special equipment.

- Functional strength development: calisthenics focuses on training multi-joint movements that involve multiple muscle groups simultaneously. This helps develop functional strength, which is essential for daily and sports activities. Calisthenics exercises train coordination and stability and improve the connection between body and mind.

- Improve flexibility and range of motion: many calisthenics exercises require a wide range of motion, which can help improve flexibility and joint mobility. For example, lunges and squats require good stretching of the legs and hips. This makes calisthenics an excellent choice for anyone who wants to improve their flexibility.

- Adaptability: calisthenics can be adapted to different fitness levels. Exercises can be made easier or more difficult by changing the angle, height, or intensity. This makes calisthenics suitable for both beginners and more experienced athletes and offers a step-by-step approach to achieving ambitious goals.

Disadvantages of Calisthenics

- Resistance limits: unlike strength training, calisthenics uses one's own body weight as resistance. While beginners can benefit significantly from training with their own body weight, more experienced athletes reach their limits in increasing strength and muscle mass without the use of additional weights.

- Complex progression: although calisthenics offers a high degree of adaptability, progression can be complex and requires a good knowledge of the exercises. It can be difficult for beginners to decide when to increase intensity or move to more difficult variations. It is important to learn basic exercise technique correctly and plan consistently to ensure proper progression.

- Limitations with certain muscle groups: Although calisthenics involves many muscle groups, it can be difficult to isolate certain muscle groups. For example, developing leg muscles can be more challenging than using traditional weights. Also, some exercise variations may work some muscle groups more than others.

- Possible limitations for muscle hypertrophy: calisthenics may promote functional strength and muscular endurance but may not be the best option for those seeking significant muscle hypertrophy. Training with additional weights and fewer repetitions may be more effective in promoting muscle growth.

Calisthenics, as we have seen, offers many benefits, but it can also have some limitations in terms of endurance, progression, and muscle building. It is important to assess your personal goals and preferences to decide whether calisthenics is suitable for your training needs.

How does an advanced athlete train in calisthenics?

The training of an advanced calisthenics athlete requires a more challenging and focused approach than that of a beginner. Advanced calisthenics athletes have already developed a solid foundation of strength, flexibility, and body control and are able to perform more complex and challenging exercises. Let's look at how calisthenics training can be structured for an advanced athlete.

Advanced calisthenics athletes benefit from advanced programming that includes a variety of exercises, progression modes, and repetition patterns. It is important to set clear and realistic goals, such as improving strength and endurance or learning new skills such as advanced lifting exercises or human flags. The program should include a combination of pulling, pushing, abdominal, and flexibility exercises, with emphasis on balance between the different muscle groups.

Focus on skills: More experienced athletes can spend more time learning and perfecting advanced calisthenic skills. These include exercises such as muscle-ups, handstand push-ups, front levers, back levers, lunges, and other advanced movements that require strength, balance, and body control. Practicing these skills takes time, patience, and dedication, but can lead to extraordinary results.

Build gradually: Even the most experienced athletes must proceed slowly with new exercises or more difficult variations. The importance of building a solid foundation and consolidating strength and stability before moving on to more advanced movements cannot be underestimated. This means that basic and intermediate exercises should be performed with maximum precision and control before moving on to more difficult variations. A smooth transition reduces the risk of injury and helps develop a solid base.

Alternation and periodization: advanced athletes may benefit from greater program variability to avoid adaptation and stagnation phenomena. This may include introducing new exercises, using different methods of progression (e.g., increasing body weight, using additional weights, or using equipment such as elastic bands), and varying training intensity, volume, and frequency. In addition, periodization, that is, training cycles with specific goals and recovery periods, can be used to maximize results.

Balance: although advanced athletes may be tempted to focus exclusively on advanced exercises, it is important to maintain a balance between strength, endurance, flexibility, and stability. This means that pulling, pushing and abdominal exercises should be included in the program in a balanced manner. In addition, the importance of flexibility and mobility training should not be overlooked to maintain adequate range of motion and prevent injury.

Finally, it is advisable to consult a qualified coach or an experienced calisthenics technician for personalized guidance and specific advice based on your needs and goals.

Structured training as an advanced calisthenics athlete requires commitment, discipline, and a solid understanding of training principles. With the right programming and approach, you can continue to reach new levels of strength, body control and skill in calisthenics.

Here is a possible advanced training plan for calisthenics. Remember that it is important to tailor your workout to your individual abilities and progress. Be sure to warm up properly before each training session and always seek advice from a fitness professional before starting a new training program.

Day 1: upper body training

- One-handed push-ups: 3 sets of 6 to 8 repetitions per arm.
- Bar pull-ups (wide grip): 3 sets of 8-10 repetitions
- Push-ups at parallel bars: 3 sets of 10-12 repetitions
- Parallel bars dips: 3 sets of 8-10 repetitions
- Squat jump with isometric stop: 3 sets of 6-8 repetitions (3-second isometric stop)
- Side plank: 3 sets of 30-60 seconds per side

Day 2: Lower body training

- Squat (Pistol): 3 sets of 6-8 repetitions per leg
- Bulgarian lunges: 3 sets of 8-10 repetitions per leg
- Squat jump: 3 sets of 10-12 repetitions (trying to jump as high as possible explosively)
- Step-up with jump: 3 sets of 8-10 repetitions per leg
- Gluteal bridge with feet on fit ball: 3 sets of 10-12 repetitions
- Side plank: 3 sets of 8-10 repetitions per leg

Day 3: Full body workout

- Muscle-up: 3 sets of 4-6 repetitions
- Standing push-ups against the wall: 3 sets of 6-8 repetitions
- Chin pulls at the barre: 3 sets of 10-12 repetitions
- Toes-to-the-bar: 4 sets 12 repetitions
- Pistol Squat: 3 sets of 6-8 reps per leg (explosive on the way up, slow and concentrated on the way down)
- Push-up Plank: 3 sets of 4-6 repetitions
- Plank : 3 sets of 30-60 seconds.

Note: The above training plan is only an example and can be modified according to your preferences and goals. Be sure to also plan enough rest days to allow your body to recover and adapt to the workout.

It is important to pay attention to proper technique in performing each exercise and gradually increase the weight and difficulty. If necessary, you can use aids such as elastic bands, heavy straps, or extra weights to adapt the exercises to your abilities.

Remember to always listen to your body and adjust the intensity and volume of your workout according to your feelings and the signals your body sends you. Proper nutrition and sufficient rest are important to support training and promote muscle growth and repair.

Let's look together at the execution of some of these exercises:

Parallel bars dips

Parallel bar dips are a calisthenics exercise that primarily works on the muscles of the upper trunk, including the triceps, pectorals, and anterior deltoids. Parallel dips are executed by using two parallel bars placed at a distance slightly greater than shoulder width apart.

Find out how to perform parallel bars dips here:

- Stand between the parallel bars with arms outstretched, keeping hands firmly on the bars. The arms should be slightly wider than the shoulders.
- Lift the body by pulling the shoulders up and away from the shoulder blades. This is the starting position. Bend your elbows and slowly lower your body, keeping your torso erect and tensing your core. Try to perform the movement in a controlled manner.
- Continue the downward movement until the elbows bend at an angle of about 90 degrees or until you feel a good stretch in the upper triceps or pectorals.
- Reverse the movement and push forcefully upward to return to the starting position, fully extending the arms.
- Repeat the movement for the desired number of repetitions.

When performing dips at the bars, make sure you have good posture with your torso upright and shoulders back. Avoid dropping your shoulders forward or bending your back too far. Keep control of your movements and breathe evenly during the exercise.
You can adjust the dips to the parallel bars according to your strength and ability. If you are a beginner, you can initially perform the exercise with your legs bent at 90 degrees to reduce the intensity. As your strength increases, you can gradually lengthen your legs or add weights to increase the challenge.

Be aware of your physical limitations and work gradually to improve strength and technique. If you suffer from shoulder or joint problems, you should consult a fitness professional or physical therapist before performing bars dip to avoid injury or complications.

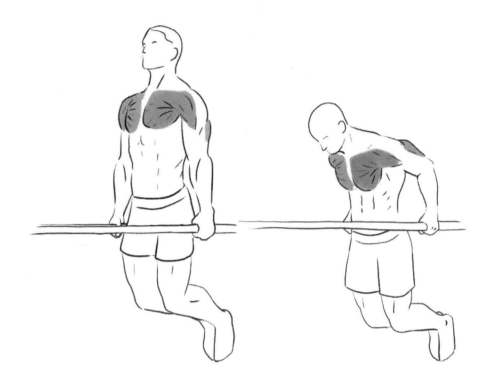

Pistol Squat

Pistol Squats are a gymnastic exercise that primarily works on the leg muscles, such as the quadriceps, glutes and ischio-crural muscles. It is an advanced variation of squats in which only one leg is used while the other remains lifted forward.

How to perform Pistol Squats.

- Stand with your feet slightly wider than shoulder width.
- Lift and extend one leg forward. Shift the weight to the opposite foot.
- Bend the knee and slowly lower the pelvis, lifting the foot forward and extending the other leg in front of you.
- Try to get as low as possible, keeping the heel of the foot raised and resting on the floor. While performing, make sure you have good posture with a straight back and an erect upper body.
- Once you reach the lowest possible point, push hard through the heel, and lift the body upward until you are back on your feet, maintaining control of the movement.
- Repeat the movement for the desired number of repetitions, then switch legs and repeat for the other leg.

When performing Pistol Squats, it is important to maintain balance and stability. To maintain balance during the exercise, you can extend your arms in front of you. You can also use a bench or chair for support to perform the exercise with a shallower depth of movement at first. As you gain strength and control, you can gradually increase the depth and perform pistol squats without support.

Pistol squats require good leg strength, balance, and flexibility. If you are a beginner, you may have to spend some time developing these qualities before you can perform the exercise correctly. Work gradually and increase the difficulty as you gain strength and body control.

As with all exercises, it is important to perform Pistol Squats with proper technique to avoid injury. If you have knee or joint problems, it is advisable to consult a fitness expert or physical therapist before performing these kinds of squats to be sure you are performing them safely and effectively.

Planche

The Planche Leans is a calisthenics exercise that aims to develop the strength and stability of the upper body, particularly the abdominal, shoulder and chest muscles. It is a more advanced exercise than the Plank, a static position in which the body is suspended horizontally in the air, the arms are extended, and the feet are off the ground.

Here is how to perform it safely:

- Bring the body into a push-up position with the hands resting on the floor at a distance slightly greater than shoulder-width apart. The fingers of the hands should be pointing forward.
- Fully extend the arms and lift the feet off the floor, stretching the body in a straight line.
- Slowly tilt the body forward by pushing the shoulders forward relative to the hands. Try to keep the body in a straight line during the tilt.
- Keep leaning forward until you feel tension in your shoulder, abdominal and chest muscles. The final position should resemble a plank with the shoulders slightly in front of the hands.
- Hold this position for a few seconds and focus on stabilizing the body and tensing the muscles involved.
- Repeat the exercise for the desired number of repetitions or hold the position for some time.

When performing planchets, it is important to have good technique and movement control. Be sure to keep your core active and tense your shoulder and abdominal muscles to keep your body stable and in line. At first you may not be able to lean very far forward, but with time and training your flexibility, strength and stability will improve.

As with all calisthenics exercises, it is important to perform this exercise safely. Be sure to warm up properly before the exercise, use a stable surface and listen to your body. If you have shoulder or joint problems, consult a fitness expert or physical therapist before performing the exercises to ensure proper execution and avoid injury.

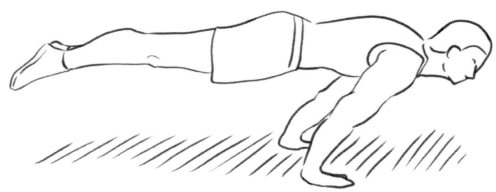

Toes to the bar

Toes-to-bar is a common exercise in gymnastics that works on the abdominals and hip flexors. The goal is to touch the bar with your toes while hanging with your arms extended. This exercise requires grip strength, core control and hip flexibility.

Find out here how to bring your toes closer to the bar:

- Stand under the bar with your arms outstretched and your hands slightly wider than shoulder width apart.
- Lean on the bar with hands in pronation grip (fingers pointing outward).

- Hold on to the bar while keeping your arms extended and your feet raised off the floor. This is the starting position.
- Contract the abdominal muscles and bend the hips while lifting the legs upward. Try to bring your toes to the bar.
- Try to stretch the legs and keep the core active during the movement. Avoid swinging or rocking your body.
- Once maximum leg elevation is reached, control the movement, and slowly lower the legs to the starting position.
- Repeat the movement for the desired number of repetitions or for the set time.
- When performing Toes-to-Bar, it is important to pay attention to proper technique to get maximum benefit and avoid injury.

Here are some points to keep in mind:

- Keep the arms extended throughout the movement to activate the abdominal and shoulder muscles to the maximum.
- Tense the core while lifting the legs to maintain stability and avoid excessive arching of the back.
- Avoid using legs or excessive rocking to perform the movement. Try to use the strength of the abdominal muscles to perform the movement slowly and in a controlled manner.

Initially you may need to perform the movement with your knees bent instead of fully extending your legs. With time and practice, you can gradually straighten your legs until they touch the bar.

The toes to the bar exercise is challenging and requires strength and coordination. If you are a beginner, you can start by performing modified versions, in which you lift your knees to your chest instead of touching the bar. As you gain strength and control, you can gradually approach the goal of performing a full exercise at the bar.

As always, it is important to perform the exercises in a safe and controlled manner. Warm up properly before the exercise, hold the bar firmly, and listen to your body. If you have shoulder or hip problems, you should consult a fitness professional or physical therapist to tailor the exercises to your needs and avoid injury.

Bulgarian lunges

Bulgarian lunges, also known as split squats, are a gymnastic exercise to strengthen and tone your lower limbs, particularly the quadriceps, glutes, and hamstrings. They take their name from Bulgaria, the country where they were originally developed.

Find out how to perform Bulgarian lunges here:

- Place one leg behind you on a bench, chair, or firm, stable surface. Position the other leg in front of you with the knee bent at 90° degrees.
- Keeping the back straight and torso erect, tense the abdominal muscles, and lower the body toward the floor by bending the knee of the front leg. The goal is to bring the back knee down without touching the floor.
- Make sure the front knee is aligned with the ankle and does not go over the toe. Keep the heel of the front leg firmly on the floor.
- Maintain a controlled stance and lower yourself until your back knee is a few inches above the floor. Be sure to maintain good balance while performing the exercise.

- Once the maximum depth is reached, push with the heel of the front leg to return to the starting position. Repeat the movement for the desired number of repetitions.

When performing Bulgarian lunges, it is important to pay attention to proper technique to maximize benefits and avoid injury.

There are some tips to keep in mind:

- Keep the torso erect and the core taut to maintain stability and proper alignment during the movement.
- Make sure the front knee is aligned with the ankle and does not go over the top of the foot to avoid undue stress on the joints.
- Work on the leg muscles by pushing the heel of the front leg upward in the concentric phase of the movement.
- You can adjust the intensity of the exercise by varying the stride length or by using additional weights such as dumbbells or kettlebells.

Bulgarian lunges offer numerous benefits, including strengthening the legs, increasing hip and core stability, and improving balance. You can incorporate them into your exercise routine to get a greater variety of leg exercises and achieve significant results in calisthenics or bodyweight training.

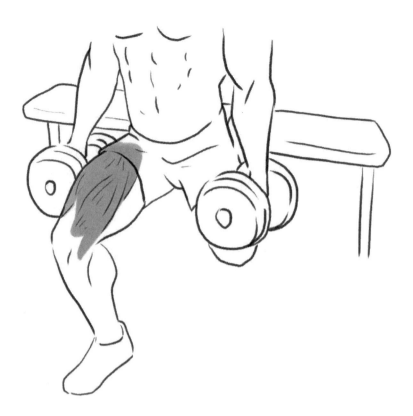

Step Up with Jump

The step-up with jump is a calisthenics exercise that combines a step-up movement with a jump, working on the leg muscles, glutes, and core stabilizing muscles. It is a dynamic exercise that improves explosive strength, balance, and coordination.

Find out how to perform the jump step-up here:

- Find a stable bench or platform at a height suitable for your fitness level. The bench should be high enough to allow you to bend your front knee at a 90-degree angle when you rest your foot.
- Stand in front of the bench and lift one foot over the bench, bending your knee and shifting your body weight to the working leg. Make sure your foot is firmly on the bench and your heel is fully supported.
- Contract your abdominal muscles and push through the heel of the working leg to lift yourself off the bench. Fully extend the leg and bring the other leg up in a jumping motion.
- During the jump, change the position of the legs by placing one leg in an outstretched position and the other on the bench.
- Land gently on the bench with the other leg and bend the knee to absorb the impact. Be sure to maintain stability and balance during the landing.
- Repeat the movement by changing legs during the jump.

When performing the jump step-up, it is important to pay attention to proper technique to avoid injury and maximize the benefits of the exercise.

A few points should be noted:

- Keep the upper body erect and the middle body tense to maintain good posture during the exercise.
- Focus on pushing upward with the active leg during the jump.
- Make sure the bench or platform on which the step-up is performed is stable and secure.
- Start with a bench or platform height that matches your fitness level and gradually increase the height if you feel more confident and efficient in performing the exercise.

The Jump Step-up is an effective exercise for improving explosive leg strength and developing coordination and balance. It can be included in your calisthenics or free body workout routine as a dynamic and fun exercise to train the legs and increase physical endurance.

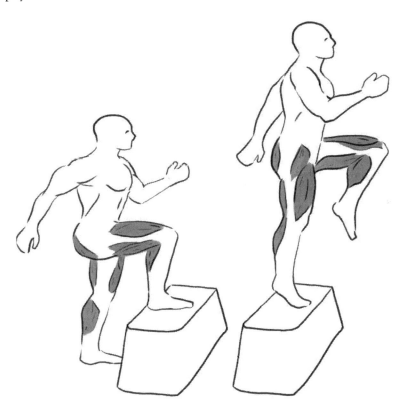

Calisthenics and Weight Loss

Metabolic benefits of Calisthenics

Calisthenics, as we have seen, is a physical activity in which the body is moved with its own body weight as resistance. The exercises activate multiple muscle groups at the same time, which requires a significant expenditure of energy. This process stimulates metabolism, which is how the body converts food into energy.

One of the main metabolic benefits of Calisthenics is increased energy expenditure during training. High-intensity calisthenics exercises require more energy than traditional resistance exercises such as weightlifting or fitness equipment. Exercises such as push-ups, lunges, squats, and burpees require many muscles in the body and their proper execution requires coordinated effort, which means more calories are consumed during the workout, which contributes to weight loss.

Another important aspect of the metabolic benefits of Calisthenics are the effects on resting metabolism. Resting metabolism is the number of calories the body burns at rest, that is, without any particular physical activity. Because Calisthenics involves building and maintaining muscle mass, it can increase this metabolism. Muscles are active tissues that consume energy even at rest. Therefore, the more muscle mass you have, the more calories you burn during the day.

Another feature that makes Calisthenics beneficial for metabolism is its ability to promote high-intensity training. For example, interval training is known to increase post-stress oxygen consumption (EPOC), that is, calorie consumption after exercise, to bring the body back to resting level. Calisthenics with its combination of cardiovascular and strength training can stimulate EPOC and prolong calorie consumption even after training.

Finally, Calisthenics offers the flexibility to tailor the intensity of exercises to your needs. Whether you are a beginner or an experienced athlete, you can adjust the intensity of the movements, number of repetitions, and recovery times to suit your specific goals. This way you can maximize the metabolic benefits of calisthenics, regardless of your initial fitness level.

In summary, the metabolic benefits of calisthenics are many. High-intensity activity and the use of muscle groups during training stimulate metabolism and increase energy expenditure both during training and at rest. In addition, high-intensity training can prolong caloric expenditure after training because of EPOC. The flexibility of Calisthenics allows you to tailor the workout to your needs, making it an effective option for those who want to lose weight and improve their metabolism.

Burn More Calories with Calisthenics

In this section we will look at some of the main calisthenics exercises that can help you burn a large number of calories.

Calisthenics is a type of high-intensity workout that effectively burns calories because it requires physical exertion, involves several muscle groups, and increases heart rate.

One of the most important calorie-burning exercises in calisthenics is the burpee. This exercise involves the whole body and combines squats, push-ups, and vertical jumps. It is a very dynamic and challenging exercise that requires coordination and strength. With a series of burpees, you can burn a large number of calories in a short time.

Another effective exercise is jumping rope. Although it seems like a simple and mundane exercise, jumping rope requires coordination, endurance, and strength. It is a high-intensity activity that stresses the muscles of the legs, buttocks, arms, and abdominals.

Push-ups are another calorie-burning exercise. The muscles of the chest, deltoid, and triceps are particularly stressed, but the abdominal muscles and stabilizing muscles of the trunk must also be involved. A large number of push-ups can be challenging and help burn calories.

Now consider lunges; this exercise involves the muscles of the legs, gluteus, and abdominals. It is a complete exercise that requires stability, strength, and coordination.

Finally, there are squats, which are one of the most important exercises in calorie-burning gymnastics. In squats, the muscles of the legs, gluteus and abdominal muscles are mainly stressed. They are a compound exercise that requires coordination and strength. A series of repeated squats can help burn calories and boost metabolism.

To burn calories with calisthenics, it is important to perform the exercises correctly and maintain high intensity during the workout. This includes performing the right number of repetitions, maintaining good form, and working at high speed, while also respecting rest times. In addition, combining exercises in high-intensity circuits can maximize caloric expenditure during training.

In summary, Calisthenics offers a wide range of exercises that allow you to burn a large number of calories. From vigorous burpees to jump ropes, push-ups, lunges, and squats-these exercises involve different muscle groups and require physical exertion. High-intensity training and proper execution of exercises are essential to maximize caloric expenditure and achieve significant weight loss results.

Proper muscle mass building with Calisthenics

Building muscle mass with calisthenics workouts is entirely possible. Although calisthenics is often thought to be primarily a discipline suitable for improving strength, endurance, and balance, it should be emphasized that it is also an excellent form of training, as many exercises target several muscle groups at once, which stimulates muscle growth evenly.

Let's take a look together at some important points to consider for increasing muscle mass with calisthenics:

Exercise progression: to stimulate muscle growth, you should apply the principle of gradual progression. This means that you should constantly challenge your muscles with increasingly difficult exercises. Start with basic exercises such as push-ups, lunges, and pull-ups, then move on to more advanced variations such as muscle-ups, pistol squats and handstand push-ups. Gradually increase the intensity, movement, and workload to progressively stimulate your muscles.

Repetitions and sets: to promote muscle hypertrophy, it is important to work with a sufficiently high load. Try to perform 8-12 repetitions per set, focusing on controlled and effective execution of each movement. Choose a reasonable number of sets to challenge your muscles, usually 3 to 5 sets per exercise.

Time under tension (TUT): time under tension refers to the total time the muscles are under tension during an exercise. To promote muscle growth, it is important to increase time under tension. You can do this by slowing down the execution of movements and maintaining muscle contraction longer. For example, you can slow down the eccentric phase of an exercise such as a push-up or a lunge.

Progressive overload: to stimulate muscle growth, you need to constantly increase the workload of your muscles. In calisthenics, you can do this through methods such as increasing the body weight used, using elastic bands, or adding additional weights through heavy backpacks or belts. For example, during pulling or pushing exercises, you can wear a heavy vest to increase the intensity and load on your muscles.

Recovery and nutrition: building muscle mass requires proper recovery and nutrition. Be sure to give your body time to recover between training sessions so that your muscles can rebuild and grow. Also, be sure to get enough protein, carbohydrates, and fats to support muscle protein synthesis and provide the nutrients needed for muscle growth.

Training variation: to avoid muscle adaptation and constantly stimulate growth, it is important to vary training. Introduce new exercises, variations, and progression modes to stimulate muscles for better results.

If you follow a proper program, apply the principles of progression, train with the right intensity, and provide your body with sufficient rest and nutrition, you can increase muscle mass with Calisthenic training. This discipline offers a wide range of exercises for different muscle groups that allow full body stimulation for muscle growth. However, it is important to know that results may vary from person to person, depending on factors such as genetics, nutrition, and commitment to training.

Finally, it is advisable to work with an experienced training professional or a calisthenics coach to develop a customized training program based on your needs and goals. A professional can help you find suitable exercises, create an appropriate progression, and provide proper technical guidance to maximize muscle-building results.

In summary, Calisthenics is an effective method of building muscle mass. By varying exercises, proper nutrition, rest, and recovery, as well as controlling the extent and intensity of training, Calisthenics as a form of training can achieve significant results in muscle building.

Development of strength and endurance with the calisthenic training method

Because calisthenics is based on using one's own body weight as resistance, it is a great way to develop functional strength. In fact, this is the key element and foundation of this discipline. Through constant movement, the body develops fluid movements and well-defined musculature. Calisthenics exercises involve multiple muscle groups simultaneously, allowing the development of balanced and functional strength in the body.

To develop strength in this discipline, it is important to choose a progressive and gradual approach. This means that you start with basic exercises and then gradually increase the intensity and level of difficulty. For example, you can start with knee push-ups or pull-ups with assistance, then move to full push-ups or pull-ups without assistance.

In addition, to develop strength, it is important to do exercises that target the major muscle groups of the body. For example, exercises such as pull-ups, push-ups, lunges, squats, and planks are excellent for strength development in the upper and lower limbs and mid-body.

In addition to strength, calisthenics also improves muscular endurance, that is, the ability of muscles to withstand longer exertion. In calisthenics, this is achieved through repeated sets of exercises with a high number of repetitions.

An important aspect of developing strength and endurance with calisthenics is proper training planning. We recommend completing a program that includes a combination of strength and endurance exercises with different intensities, volumes, and repetitions. An instructor or training expert can help create a tailored program that takes into account individual skills and goals.

In addition, it is important to pay attention to the proper execution of exercises to maximize the impact on strength and endurance. Proper technique is essential to ensure proper muscle activation and avoid injury. Proper technical guidance from a professional can be of great help to ensure that you perform the exercises correctly.

Finally, it is important to include periods of rest and recovery in training so that the body can adapt to stimuli and recover properly. Rest is important to avoid overtraining and to allow muscles to rebuild and grow.

In summary, calisthenics offers a great way to develop strength and endurance. With a progressive approach, proper programming, correct exercise execution, and sufficient breaks, significant results in strength and endurance can be achieved with calisthenics as a form of training.

Improved mobility

Mobility is an essential aspect of Calisthenics, as it enables proper execution of exercises, reduces the risk of injury, and promotes greater freedom of movement. Good mobility allows you to assume wider stances and perform exercises with a wider range of motion, which can increase the effectiveness of your workout.

To improve agility, several strategies can be used. First, it is important to include specific exercises in your training program. Static stretching exercises such as chest or back stretches, butterfly stretches, glute stretches, and triceps stretches can be performed before and after training to improve muscle flexibility.

In addition, joint mobility exercises can be used to increase the range of motion of the joints involved in calisthenics exercises. For example, exercises such as dynamic lunges and spinal rotations can help improve body mobility and elasticity.

It is important to spend time on each exercise so that the muscles can gradually relax and stretch. Hold each stretching position for at least 20 to 30 seconds and breathe deeply to promote muscle relaxation.

In addition to mobility exercises, progressive training can be used to improve mobility. For example, advanced variations of exercises that require increased flexibility, such as splits, bridges, or planks, can help stimulate muscle lengthening and improve flexibility over time.

It is important to know that flexibility is a gradual process that requires perseverance and patience.
Finally, it is important to pay attention to proper technique when performing calisthenics exercises. Poor technique can limit mobility and increase the risk of injury. If you pay attention to performing the exercises with good posture, proper body alignment, and controlled breathing, you can improve your flexibility and execution of the exercises.

How to improve balance and stability

Balance is a crucial element in calisthenics, as it allows you to maintain a stable and controlled posture during exercises. With good balance, exercises such as planks, handstand push-ups and pistol squats can be performed more easily and effectively.

There are several strategies for improving balance with calisthenics. One of the most important is the inclusion of specific balance exercises in the training program. Balance exercises can be performed both statically and dynamically and involve controlling the body in unstable positions.

A common exercise to improve balance is the "One-leg balance" in which you try to balance on one leg for a period of time. This exercise can be complicated by closing your eyes or performing it on an unstable support such as a pillow or padding.

Another effective exercise is the handstand, in which you try to keep your balance as long as possible. This exercise requires a high level of stability and control of the body requiring strength and balance.

For the development of balance, it is important to train the stabilizing muscles of the body, such as the muscles of the trunk, lower limbs, and upper body. Exercises such as planks, side lunges, and pull-ups can help strengthen these muscles and improve overall balance.
In addition, regular practice of yoga or Pilates can be helpful in improving balance in calisthenics. These disciplines focus on posture alignment, body awareness, and breathing control, all of which are important for balance.

It is important to know that developing balance takes time, patience, and constant practice. If you start with easier balance exercises and gradually increase the level of difficulty, you can develop good stability over time.

Finally, it is always important to pay attention to proper technique when performing calisthenics exercises that require balance. Good posture, correct body alignment, and proper breathing control can lead to better balance and more confidence when performing the exercises.
Balance is therefore a crucial aspect of calisthenics. By including specific exercises, strengthening stabilizing muscles, and practicing regularly, it is possible to improve overall balance with calisthenics, this allows for better execution of exercises and more satisfactory training results.

Developing Resilience

Endurance is a key element of Calisthenics as it allows you to perform a series of repetitions of exercises without getting tired too quickly. Good endurance allows you to maintain a high level of performance during training and to perform more sets and repetitions.

To improve endurance, several strategies can be applied. One of the most important is to include high-intensity exercises, low weights, and a high number of repetitions in training. This type of training promotes the development of muscular and cardiovascular endurance.

For example, exercises such as push-ups, bar pulls, squats and lunges can be performed in high-intensity sequences, alternating the various exercises without longer breaks. This type of training, so-called circuit training, allows complete stimulation of the muscular and cardiovascular systems.

Another approach to endurance development in Calisthenics is interval training. Short intensive training sessions are performed, followed by active or full recovery phases. For example, you can alternate between high-intensity exercises such as burpees, climbers, and jumping jacks, followed by short recovery periods.

You can also do time-based training in which you perform exercises for a certain period of time, trying to maintain a steady pace and doing as many repetitions as possible. This type of training helps improve muscular endurance and the ability to maintain effort for a longer period of time.

It is important to remember that resistance development requires a gradual progression. Start with a reasonable number of repetitions and appropriate intensity and increase it over time. This way the body can gradually adapt to the training and the risk of injury is reduced.

In addition to specific exercises, it is important to pay attention to nutrition and hydration. A proper diet with a balanced nutrient ratio and adequate hydration during training are key factors in maintaining physical endurance and achieving optimal results.
Finally, for endurance development in calisthenics, it is critical to take time to rest. Breaks allow the body to regenerate and adapt to training, enabling better performance and preventing the occurrence of fatigue and overtraining.

The development of endurance during Calisthenics training is an essential condition for performing more intense and longer exercises. It is possible to improve overall endurance and it is very satisfying to achieve better results during Calisthenics training.

Improving joint mobility with Calisthenics

Flexibility is an important aspect of Calisthenics because it enables exercises with a wide range of motion, promotes better posture, and reduces the risk of muscle strain and injury.

Several strategies can be used to improve mobility during calisthenics training. One of the most important is the inclusion of static stretching exercises in the training routine. During static stretching, the muscles are stretched into a position that is held for a period of time so that they can gradually relax and lengthen.

Some examples of static stretching exercises suitable for calisthenics are the "squat hold" in which you squat down and hold the position for 30-60 seconds, the "straddle stretch" in which you open your legs in a split position and hold the position for 30-60 seconds, and the "Chest Stretch" in which you stretch your arms, stretch your chest, and hold the position for 30-60 seconds.

It is important to perform static stretching exercises correctly without overstretching the muscles. It is recommended to warm up before starting to stretch and to breathe deeply during stretching to promote muscle relaxation.

In addition to static stretching, it is useful to include joint mobility exercises in the program. Joint mobility includes the controlled movement of joints over their full range of motion. Joint mobility exercises can help improve the flexibility and stability of joints involved in calisthenics exercises.

For example, exercises such as "Cat-Camel-Stretch" is perfect for the spine, shoulder and hip rotation and it can be used to improve joint mobility and promote better execution of calisthenics exercises.

In addition, it is important to gradually improve flexibility. Start with basic stretching and agility exercises and increase the intensity and duration of stretches over time.

Stability is a key element in improving mobility in calisthenics. During each training session, it is recommended that specific time is devoted to stretching and agility and that active recovery is an integral part of the routine to promote muscle recovery and overall flexibility.

Mistakes to avoid in calisthenics

Lack of warming up

Insufficient warm-up before Calisthenics training is a common mistake that can affect performance, increase the risk of injury, and limit training results. Warming up is important to prepare the body and mind for intense physical activity. The following are some points to consider to avoid this mistake:

Increased body temperature: Warming up aims to increase body temperature and blood circulation, resulting in better flow of oxygen and nutrients to the muscles. This promotes lubrication of joints, increases elasticity of muscle tissues and tendons, and prepares the body for high-intensity physical activities.

Muscle preparation: warm-up is used to activate the muscles that are being worked on during training. Mobility exercises and specific movements can prepare the muscles for the upcoming activity. In Calisthenics, for example, it can be useful to perform dynamic stretching exercises to lengthen the main muscles involved such as shoulders, back, arms, legs, and trunk.

Performance enhancement: proper warm-up can improve performance during training. Gradually increasing the intensity and amplitude of movements during the warm-up allows the body to gradually adapt to the next physical activity. This helps improve strength, endurance, and coordination in Calisthenics exercises.

Reduced risk of injury: proper warm-up can help prevent muscle, tendon, and joint injuries. Increased body temperature and improved tissue elasticity reduce the load and tension on muscles and joints, making sprains, muscle tears, or other workout-related injuries less likely.

Mental preparation: warming up is not only about the body, but also about the mind. Taking the time to mentally focus on the upcoming workout, visualizing movements and mentally preparing for physical exertion can help improve concentration and motivation during training.
It is important to use at least 10-15 minutes of complete warm-up before Calisthenics training. This can include dynamic stretching exercises, joint mobility exercises, muscle activation exercises, and specific movements to properly prepare the body. In addition, it is always advisable to consult a professional trainer or Calisthenics teacher for guidance tailored to your fitness level and goals.

Improper technique during exercises

Proper technique is essential in gymnastics to achieve optimal results and avoid injury. Errors in exercise technique can often compromise the effectiveness of the movement and jeopardize the safety of the athlete.

Here are some important points to consider to ensure proper technique during gymnastics:

Body alignment: it is important to maintain good body alignment during exercises. Make sure the spine is in a neutral position, the shoulders are relaxed, and the knees do not protrude beyond the toes. Proper alignment reduces the risk of injury and optimizes the effectiveness of exercise.

Trunk control: the trunk, composed of abdominal, back, and pelvic muscles, is critical for body stability and control during calisthenics exercises. Be sure to activate and stretch your core appropriately with each movement, tensing your abdomen slightly and keeping your back straight.

Maximum Range of Motion: try to perform exercises with a wide range of motion, making maximum use of joint extensibility and flexibility. Avoid partial or restricted movements that may limit the benefits of the exercise and increase the risk of muscle imbalances.

Proper breathing: proper breathing during exercises is important to maintain good control and stability. Try to breathe regularly and in a controlled manner by exhaling during the tension phase and breathing out during the relaxation phase.

Gradual increase: it is important to gradually increase the difficulty levels of calisthenics exercises. Do not try advanced movements until you have gained a good base of strength and control. Start with simpler variations of the exercises and gradually increase the complexity and intensity as your skills improve.

Supervision and feedback: supervision by an experienced coach or Calisthenics teacher can be extremely helpful in ensuring proper technique. A trained eye can detect errors in your execution and give you valuable feedback for improvement.

Video recording: another useful tool for assessing technique is recording your training sessions. Use a smartphone or camera to film yourself during your workout and then carefully evaluate your form. You can note any mistakes that need to be corrected or techniques that can be improved.

Proper technique in Calisthenics exercises takes time, practice, and body awareness. Take the time to learn and perfect basic technique before moving on to more complex exercises. Performing the exercises correctly not only maximizes your results, but also helps you prevent injury and improve your overall fitness.

Overtraining

Now, we will address the risk of overtraining in Calisthenics and the importance of proper rest and recovery planning to avoid injury and achieve optimal results.

Calisthenics is an intense physical activity that requires a lot of effort and commitment. However, it is important to strike a balance between training and recovery to ensure long-term success and avoid physical and mental exhaustion.

The following are some important points to keep in mind to avoid overtraining during gymnastics:

Plan your training program: it is important to develop a well-structured training program that includes phases of appropriate intensity and range, recovery days or low-intensity activities. Find the right balance between training and recovery, considering your fitness level, goals, and recovery capacity.

Listen to your body: pay attention to the signals your body sends you. If you feel tired and exhausted or have persistent muscle aches, it could be a sign of overtraining. Pay attention to your body's signals and take time to rest and recover when you need to.

Active rest: rest does not necessarily mean sitting completely still and doing nothing. Active recovery can also be an effective strategy to promote recovery. You can do low-intensity activities such as yoga, stretching, light walking or mobility exercises to stimulate blood circulation, relieve muscle tension and promote recovery.

Good sleep quality: sleep is a key element of recovery. Make sure you get good, quality sleep every night. During sleep, the body regenerates and repairs itself, allowing muscles and tissues to recover from training efforts.

Proper nutrition: a balanced, nutrient-rich diet is essential for training and recovery during calisthenics training. Be sure to take in a variety of nutrients, including carbohydrates, protein, healthy fats, vitamins, and minerals, to support muscle recovery and overall health.

Intensity reduction: it is important to periodically include phases of intensity reduction in training. These periods allow the body to recover, adapt and regenerate better. You can plan low-tonnage, low-volume weeks by reducing the intensity or volume of exercises so that the body can recover and adapt optimally.

Training Variation: avoid monotony during training by varying movements, sequences, and goals. Variety can help prevent mental and physical wear and tear, keep motivation high, and stimulate the body in different ways.

Professional advice: if you have concerns about planning your training program or proper recovery, you should contact an experienced fitness professional or a calisthenics coach. They can offer you personalized advice based on your specific needs and goals.

Avoiding overtraining with calisthenics is critical to maintaining health, improving performance, and achieving lasting results. Respect your body, plan your training wisely, and make recovery a priority to maximize the benefits of calisthenics.

Insufficient recovery

As we've just said, proper recovery is critical to Calisthenics success. During training, your body is overloaded and muscle tissue microinjuries occur. In the resting phase, your body repairs and strengthens muscles so you can achieve better long-term results.

The following are some tips to avoid mistakes related to insufficient recovery at Calisthenics:

Rest breaks too short between training sessions: plan regular rest days between training sessions. Then, your body can recover, repair damaged tissues, and become stronger. Avoid training the same muscle groups several days in a row by giving them time to recover. A forty-eight-hour break is recommended.

Sufficient sleep: sleep is critical for muscle recovery, tissue repair and energy recovery. Try to get at least 7-9 hours of quality sleep each night. Provide a conducive sleeping environment in a dark room with a cool temperature and a comfortable bed.

Balanced nutrition: a healthy, balanced diet provides the body with the nutrients it needs for muscle recovery and rebuilding. Be sure to take in enough protein to support muscle protein synthesis, carbohydrates to restore glycogen stores, and healthy fats for energy supply.

Active recovery activities: in addition to rest, you can include active recovery activities in your routine, such as stretching, muscle relaxation, joint movement and breathing. These activities promote blood circulation, reduce muscle tension, and aid recovery.

Stress management: chronic stress can negatively affect calisthenics recovery and performance. Find healthy ways to manage stress, such as meditation, yoga, reading or listening to relaxing music. Also practice daily stress management with techniques such as deep breathing and muscle relaxation.

Avoid overtraining: this can lead to chronic fatigue, injury, and a decline in performance. Pay attention to your body's signals and don't overtrain. Maintain a balance between intensity and duration of training sessions and leave room for recovery.

Listen to your body: each person has individual recovery needs; listen to your body and respond to its needs. If you feel tired and unmotivated, it may be a sign that you need more recovery time. Respect your limits and don't be afraid to take the time to recover properly.

Proper recovery during calisthenics training is critical to improving strength, endurance, and overall performance. Take care of your body, give it the recovery time it needs, and you will experience the best training results.

Lack of progression and variety of exercises

One of the keys to achieving results with Calisthenics is to gradually increase the exercises. Progression means that the difficulty level and intensity of the exercises gradually increase over time. So, your body can gradually adapt and develop strength and skill.

The following are some common mistakes to avoid in terms of progression and variability in Calisthenics training:

Skipping progression levels: many people are impatient and tend to skip early progression levels. For example, they try to do instant pull-ups without first developing the necessary strength. This can increase the risk of injury and prevent effective progression. Be sure to progress gradually, starting with basic exercises and continuing only with increasing strength and control.

No variation of exercises: it is important to bring variety into your exercise program and modify your exercises. If you limit yourself to the same exercises over and over again, your body will adapt, and you may reach a physiological stalemate. Experiment with exercise variations, such as changing the angle, range of motion, or using additional equipment to stimulate your muscles in new ways.

Don't work on your weaknesses: every person has weaknesses and areas they need to focus on more to make improvements. Ignoring these weaknesses can limit your progress in gymnastics. Identify your weaknesses and record specific exercises on them. For example, if you have difficulty with push-ups, you might spend time improving shoulder strength or core stability.

Track your progress: it is important to monitor your progress in Calisthenics training to make sure you are constantly improving. Keep a record of the exercises you perform, the number of repetitions, and the variations you apply. This way you can see your progress and, if necessary, modify your training program.

Don't tailor the program to your goals: if you pursue specific calisthenics goals, such as increasing strength, improving muscle hypertrophy, or developing endurance, it is important to adjust your training program accordingly. Be sure to choose the exercises and progression mode that best suit your goals.

Neglect form and technique: proper form and technique are critical to avoid injury and maximize results. Be sure to perform the exercises correctly while maintaining good posture, sufficient stability, and complete control of movement. If necessary, work with a qualified trainer to learn proper exercise technique.

Gradual increase and sufficient training variability are the keys to success. Avoid the common mistakes listed above and be sure to follow a well-structured training program that takes into account the principles of progression and variability to achieve the best possible results.

Lack of proper Monitoring and Professional Counseling

Calisthenics requires good knowledge of technique and proper exercise form, as well as proper progression and programming to achieve one's goals. Below are some common mistakes due to lack of professional assistance and advice at Calisthenics:

Improper exercise execution: without proper supervision, one can easily fall into poor exercise technique. This can cause injury, slow progress, and affect desired results. It is important to work with a qualified instructor or experienced coach who will guide you in the proper execution of exercises and correct technical errors.

No structured sequence: the sequence of Calisthenics exercises is critical to achieve results. Without a proper program, you can perform the same exercises repeatedly without making significant improvements. An experienced professional can help you develop a structured sequence so that you can progress gradually and safely.

Lack of workout program adaptation: each person has different needs and abilities, and what is good for one is not necessarily right for another. By working with a Calisthenics expert, you can tailor your training program to your specific needs, goals, and fitness levels. This way you can maximize results and reduce the risk of injury.

Inattention of stress test impact: Calisthenics relies on stress test impact, that is, the gradual increase in resistance or difficulty of exercises over time. Without proper supervision, you can fall into the trap of always performing the same number of repetitions or the same variation of exercises without increasing. A professional can help you determine the right load and plan gradual increase to continually stimulate your muscles for lasting results.

Lack of motivation and accountability: training alone can sometimes lead to a lack of motivation and accountability. Working with a coach or a group of people pursuing the same goals can help you maintain your motivation, stick to your training program, and overcome any obstacles that may arise along the way.

Professional assistance and advice are essential in Calisthenics to achieve the best results in terms of fitness, progress, and safety. Do not hesitate to contact a qualified professional who can accompany you on your training journey and tailor the program to your specific needs and goals.

Lack of patience and perseverance

Calisthenics is a sport that requires time, dedication, and perseverance. Here are some common mistakes related to lack of patience and perseverance:

Expect immediate results: many people start Calisthenics and expect immediate results. However, building strength, endurance and muscle takes time. It is important to realize that Calisthenics results are progressive and require consistent commitment over a long period of time.

Skipping the learning phase: in Calisthenics it is important to take the time to properly learn the technique and form of the exercises. Skipping this phase can result in execution errors and possible injury. It is important to acquire a solid foundation of knowledge and skills through gradual learning and repeated practice.

Focus exclusively on the external result: Calisthenics is not only about appearance, but also about building strength, flexibility, and body control. Focusing exclusively on outward appearance can lead to a lack of long-term satisfaction and motivation. It is also important to celebrate small progressions and celebrate advances in strength, endurance, and technical skills.

Surrender in the face of difficulty: in calisthenics there will always be moments of challenge and frustration. You may come across exercises that seem impossible to perform or achieve a level of progress. It is critical to maintain perseverance and view difficulties as opportunities for growth. Perseverance in overcoming obstacles will help you reach higher levels of performance in Calisthenics training.

You don't take the time to evaluate and adapt your training program: in Calisthenics it is important to regularly evaluate your progress and adapt your training program accordingly. If you get stuck or don't see significant improvement, you may need to adjust your intensity, exercise variety, or training volume. Patience and the ability to adapt to your body's needs are essential in making progress.

Patience and perseverance are key elements to achieve lasting results and reaching your goals. Don't let challenges and slow progress discourage you. Remember that Calisthenics is a journey of personal growth and that every small step counts. Be patient, persistent and trust your path and the results will come soon.

Calisthenics vs. Strength Training

Calisthenics and strength training are two different approaches to improve strength and fitness. Let's take a look at the main characteristics of the two:

Calisthenics:

- Body weight is used as the main resistance during exercises.
- The exercises are based on functional and natural movements, such as pull-ups, push-ups, squats, and lunges.
- Promotes the development of balance, coordination, and flexibility.
- It can be practiced anywhere without the need for special equipment or visiting a gym.
- Offers a wide range of exercises and progressions for different fitness levels.
- It stimulates multiple muscle groups simultaneously and improves stability and overall strength.
- It requires mastery of movement and good technique to achieve effective results.
- It may be suitable for those seeking functional and dynamic training without pursuing the goal of building large muscle mass.

Strength training:

- Use external weights such as dumbbells and machines to create resistance during exercises.
- You can isolate specific muscle groups to develop them in a targeted way.
- It promotes increased muscle mass and strength, especially when a progressive weightlifting protocol is applied.
- Provides greater ability to vary intensity and workload according to individual needs and goals.
- Requires access to a gym or suitable environment with special equipment.
- It is important to learn proper technique and safety in performing the exercises to avoid injury.
- It may be suitable for those who wish to achieve significant gains in muscle mass or focus on specific muscle groups.

Both approaches have their advantages and can be integrated into a comprehensive program. The choice depends on personal preferences, individual goals, and available resources. Some people choose a combination of calisthenics and strength training to achieve a balance of muscle building, strength, and function.

Calisthenics vs. Free Body Workout

Calisthenics and free-body training are two similar approaches based on the use of body weight as the main resistance. Let's take a look at the main characteristics of the two:

Calisthenics:

- Calisthenics is a discipline that includes a wide range of free-body exercises, such as pull-ups, push-ups, squats, lunges, and many other variations.
- Emphasis is on functional movements that respond to multiple muscle groups simultaneously.
- It promotes balance, coordination, and flexibility, as well as muscle strength and endurance.
- Calisthenics offers a wide range of exercises and progressions that allow training to be tailored to different fitness levels and goals.
- It can be practiced anywhere without the need for special equipment or visiting a gym.
- It requires good technique and control of movement to achieve effective results.
- It may be suitable for those seeking functional and dynamic training without pursuing the goal of building large muscle mass.

Free body workout:

- Free-body training is a training approach in which one's own body weight is used as resistance without the help of equipment or machines.
- Free-body exercises can include push-ups, pull-ups, arm bends, squats, lunges, planks, and many other variations.
- The main goal of free-body training is to develop strength, muscular endurance, and body tension.
- Free body training allows for a wide range of exercises involving different muscle groups.
- It can be practiced anywhere without the need for special equipment or visiting a gym.
- It requires good technique and control of movement to achieve effective results.
- It may be suitable for those seeking functional training without the goal of building large muscle mass.

Both approaches offer significant benefits for strength, endurance, and overall fitness. The choice between calisthenics and free-body training depends on personal preferences, individual goals, and available resources. Both can effectively improve muscle strength, balance, and coordination. Both approaches can be integrated into a comprehensive training program to achieve more variety and muscle stimulation.

Calisthenics and Meditation

Calisthenics and meditation are two practices that, despite different goals and approaches, can complement each other to provide both physical and mental benefits. Let's consider in detail how these two disciplines are related and how they can enrich your practice.

Calisthenics focuses on strength training with one's own body weight as resistance. Calisthenics exercises such as pull-ups, push-ups, lunges, and balance exercises require concentration, coordination, and body mastery. The main goal of calisthenics is to develop strength, muscular endurance, flexibility, and agility.

Meditation, on the other hand, is a practice that focuses on perceiving the present moment and observing thoughts, feelings, and emotions. Through meditation, one seeks to cultivate a calm, focused and balanced mind, relieve stress and increase mental well-being.

Despite the obvious differences, calisthenics and meditation can be integrated synergistically; here's how it works:

Body awareness: Calisthenics and meditation promote body awareness. In Calisthenics, concentration on body movement and posture during exercises promotes body awareness. Meditation focuses on body sensations, so as to develop greater awareness of body signals.

Mental concentration: both exercises require mental concentration. In calisthenics, focusing on performing the exercises correctly and overcoming physical limitations requires a focused mind. Meditation develops the ability to focus attention on a particular object, such as the breath or a repeated word or phrase, increasing mental clarity and the ability to concentrate.

Stress management: calisthenics and meditation can help reduce stress and promote mental well-being. The intensive exercises of Calisthenics can relieve tensions and fears accumulated in the body, while meditation helps cultivate mindfulness and inner calm, relieve stress, and improve emotional management.

Presence in the present moment: both calisthenics and meditation invite one to be present in the moment. Calisthenics focuses on performing the exercises correctly without being distracted by thoughts or worries. In meditation, one practices being present and perceiving what is happening in the present moment, without judging or attempting to control thoughts.

Integration of body and mind: calisthenics and meditation promote the integration of body and mind. In calisthenics, fluid and coordinated movements require harmony between body and mind. Meditation develops awareness of the connection between mind and body, recognizing the mutual influence of the two.

It is important to note that meditation don't need be done at the same time as calisthenics training. It can be done at a separate time, perhaps before or after the workout, to gain the specific mental benefits of meditation.

In summary, calisthenics and meditation can be synergistically integrated to improve physical and mental well-being. Both practices promote mindfulness, mental focus, and stress management. The combination of these two disciplines can lead to a more comprehensive and rewarding practice that enables the development of a strong, mobile body and a calm, balanced mind.

Calisthenics for mental health: psychological benefits

Calisthenics not only offers physical benefits but can also have a significant impact on mental health and well-being. Here are some of the psychological benefits calisthenics can offer:

Stress reduction: exercise, including calisthenics, has been shown to have a significant impact on mental health and can be an effective strategy for reducing stress and anxiety.

During physical activity such as calisthenics, the body releases endorphins - neurotransmitters known for their positive effect on psychological well-being. Endorphins act as natural pain relievers and improve mood by transmitting a feeling of euphoria and well-being. This can help reduce stress accumulated during the day and relieve anxiety.

In addition, calisthenics can provide a form of "release" from accumulated negative emotions. During training, we can transform tensions and fears into intense and focused physical movements. This allows us to release accumulated tensions in the body and mind and create a feeling of relief and lightness.

Scientific studies have shown the effectiveness of exercise in reducing stress and anxiety. For example, a systematic review published in 2019 examined 16 clinical studies and concluded that exercise, including Calisthenics, can significantly reduce anxiety symptoms. In addition, a 2018 study found that exercise can be as effective in reducing anxiety as psychological interventions.

In addition to releasing endorphins, calisthenics can also promote the release of other chemicals in the brain that have a positive effect on mental well-being. For example, the production of serotonin, a neurotransmitter that regulates mood and conveys a feeling of calm and happiness, is stimulated.

A practical example would be a person participating in a calisthenics training session after a stressful day at work. During the workout, the person who focuses on different movements and pursues new goals may experience a reduction in stress level and an improvement in mood. At the end of the workout, one feels more relaxed, satisfied, and ready to face daily challenges in a more positive way.

In summary, calisthenics offers a unique way to relieve stress and anxiety through movement. By releasing endorphins, serotonin and other physiological benefits, Calisthenics can help improve mental well-being and promote a feeling of calm and happiness.

Increased self-esteem and self-confidence: let's take a look at how calisthenics can contribute to this process of personal growth:

Overcoming challenges: Calisthenics requires facing and overcoming various physical challenges. So, for example, it may be difficult to do a series of push-ups or perform a number of pull-ups at the bar. However, through constant practice and a willingness to improve your skills, you can overcome these challenges. Each time you overcome an obstacle, you increase your self-confidence and promote self-esteem. This leads to a greater awareness of your abilities and the belief that you can achieve ambitious goals.

Visible progress: One of the benefits of Calisthenics is that the results are visible in the body and physical abilities. Consistent training allows one to observe improvements in strength, balance, flexibility, and muscle definition. This tangible progress helps increase self-esteem and self-confidence. The certainty of being able to perform an exercise that previously seemed impossible or of having achieved a certain desired physical form leads to increased confidence in one's abilities.

Personal performance: achieving goals in Calisthenics leads to a sense of personal accomplishment. For example, this may be the ability to perform a certain advanced exercise such as muscle-ups or increasing personal hang time at the bar. These achievements not only boost self-confidence but also create pride. Knowing that you have invested time, effort, and perseverance to achieve these milestones builds confidence in your own abilities.

Supportive communities: Calisthenics provides a social environment where calisthenics enthusiasts can share their experiences, support each other, and celebrate success. Online communities or offline training groups can provide moral support and encouragement toward self-improvement. Interacting with others who share the same passion and goals helps create a sense of belonging and confidence in one's journey.

Skills transfer: the successful experiences and self-confidence gained from Calisthenics can have a positive impact on other areas of life. The discipline, commitment, and determination developed during training can be transferred to areas such as work, study, or personal relationships. This self-confidence and ability to cope with challenges is reflected in overall self-esteem and in everyday life.

Ultimately, calisthenics can help boost self-esteem and self-confidence by overcoming challenges, visible progress, improved personal achievements, community support, and transfer of skills to other areas of life. Together, these factors can lead to greater confidence in one's abilities, a more positive view of oneself, and greater confidence in achieving one's goals.

Increased mental energy: what can Calisthenics do?

Improved concentration: calisthenics training requires good concentration to perform exercises correctly, control breathing and maintain proper form. This focused attention requires mental effort that stimulates the brain and improves the ability to concentrate. A study published in the journal Psychology of Sport and Exercise shows that calisthenics training can improve concentration and cognitive function.

Stress reduction: Calisthenics can serve as a form of reducing accumulated stress. During exercise, endorphins, the so-called "happy hormones," are released, which help reduce stress and promote a general feeling of psychological well-being. In addition, physical training can distract the mind from negative thoughts and promote the production of neurotransmitters such as serotonin, which help improve mood and mental energy.

Cognitive stimulation: Calisthenics requires coordination, memory and information processing that stimulate brain activity. For example, when learning a new sequence of movements or trying to improve the technique of an exercise, different areas of the brain involved in learning and information processing are activated. A study published in the Journal of Aging and Physical Activity showed that physical activity, including calisthenics, can improve cognitive functions, including attention, memory, and information processing.

Increased mental resilience: Calisthenics requires commitment, patience, and perseverance to achieve one's goals. Through continued practice, one develops greater mental resilience, that is, the ability to cope with difficulties, overcome obstacles and get back up after a defeat. This resilience can be transferred to other areas of life, enabling one to face daily challenges with greater determination and mental strength.

Sense of personal fulfillment: achieving goals in Calisthenics, such as performing an advanced exercise or improving one's skills, leads to a sense of personal accomplishment. This feeling of achievement and satisfaction increases mental energy, boosts motivation, and creates a sense of self-esteem and self-confidence.

Finally, Calisthenics can help increase mental energy through increased concentration, stress reduction, cognitive stimulation, increased mental load capacity, and a sense of personal fulfillment. These benefits can improve overall mental well-being, promote optimal mental health, and improve quality of life.

Improving emotional well-being: let's take a look at what Calisthenics can do:

Anxiety and stress reduction: exercise, including Calisthenics, is known for its positive effects on reducing anxiety and stress. Sports release endorphins, which improve mood and reduce anxiety.

Increasing self-esteem: Calisthenics provides opportunities to achieve new goals and overcome personal challenges. Consistently working to improve one's physical abilities and overcome one's limitations can lead to increased self esteem and self-confidence. The sense of personal accomplishment and progress in achieving Calisthenics goals can have a significant impact on emotional well-being.

Improved mood: movement is associated with improved mood because of the release of neurotransmitters such as endorphins and serotonin, which are responsible for positive feelings and emotional well-being. Regular Calisthenics workouts can contribute to overall mood improvement and greater emotional stability over time.

Reduction in depressive symptoms: Physical activity, including Calisthenics, is associated with a reduction in depressive symptoms. A study published in the Journal of Clinical Psychology showed that exercise has a significant antidepressant effect and can be used as part of depression treatment. Consistent activity can convey structure and a sense of intentionality, which can help improve overall emotional well-being.

Emotional stress management: Calisthenics can serve as a form of emotional stress management by providing an opportunity for distraction and an outlet for negative emotions. The focused attention required while performing the exercises can help clear the mind of stressful thoughts and focus on the body and movement. In addition, the exercises stimulate the production of endorphins, which can convey a feeling of calm and emotional well-being. In summary, Calisthenics can help improve emotional well-being by reducing anxiety and stress, increasing self-esteem, improving mood, reducing depressive symptoms, and addressing emotional stress. These benefits can have a significant impact on mental health and improve overall quality of life.

Managing mood swings: let's look in detail at how calisthenics can contribute to this benefit:

Mood regulation: movement, including Calisthenics, has been shown to have positive effects on mood regulation. Neurotransmitters, known to improve mood and promote well-being, are released during physical activity. This can be especially helpful for people suffering from mood disorders such as depression or bipolar disorder.

Reducing symptoms of anxiety and depression: Calisthenics can help reduce symptoms of anxiety and depression. Regular exercise is associated with a reduction in anxiety and depressive symptoms. A study conducted at the University of Toronto found that exercise can be as effective in moderate depression as traditional therapies. Calisthenics offers an affordable and accessible way to get moving and benefit from the positive effects on mental health.

Increased positive neurotransmitters: during gymnastics, the body produces a number of neurotransmitters that influence mood and emotional well-being. A study published in the Journal of Psychiatric Research shows that sports stimulate the production of neurotransmitters such as dopamine and norepinephrine, which are associated with positive mood and motivation. This can help improve mood and cope with mood disorders.

Distraction and mental focus: during Calisthenics practice, the focus is on performing the exercises and moving the body. This can distract from worries and negative thoughts that can promote mood disorders. In addition, the exercise requires mental concentration, which creates a kind of "break" from the mind and allows you to get rid of stressful thoughts.

Experience success and self-confidence: Calisthenics provides opportunities to achieve new goals and constantly improve one's physical abilities. These personal successes can lead to successful experiences and boost self-confidence, which is important in the treatment of mood disorders. Progress in Calisthenics and overcoming one's limits can improve self-esteem and provide a positive boost to the management of mood disorders.

In summary, Calisthenics can be an effective option for treating mood disorders. By regulating mood, reducing symptoms of anxiety and depression, increasing positive neurotransmitters, mental distraction and concentration, and a sense of contentment and self-worth, calisthenics can help improve overall emotional well-being and promote better management of mood disorders.

Propaedeutics

Propaedeutics play a key role in preparing the body for more advanced exercises in Calisthenics. This chapter covers propaedeutics as an integral part of a training program. You will learn how important it is, the main goals it pursues, and how to implement them effectively.

Calisthenics precursors play a key role in the training process because they provide a solid foundation for performing advanced and complex exercises. Here are the significance and goals of the precursors:

Technique improvement: With calisthenics propaedeutics you can learn and perfect the right technique for exercises. This is a prerequisite for safe and effective execution of advanced calisthenics exercises. Learning good posture, proper body alignment and controlled movements helps to avoid injury and optimize results.

Basic strength development: Basic propaedeutics in calisthenics aims to strengthen the stabilizing muscles and muscle groups involved in performing the more complex exercises. This contributes to stabilizing the body and improving overall strength. Solid trunk strength development is important to sustain and progress in the more challenging exercises such as pull-ups, handstand push-ups, and human flags.

Improving mobility and flexibility: Calisthenics propaedeutics often include joint mobility and stretching exercises that improve joint range of motion. Good mobility and flexibility are essential to perform calisthenics exercises correctly and avoid muscle or joint injuries.

Balance and coordination development: many calisthenics propaedeutics require good balance and coordination to perform the exercises in a stable and controlled manner. Training with Calisthenics propaedeutics improves these skills, which are critical for performing complex movements and supporting one's body weight in different positions.

Gradual increase: propaedeutic calisthenics provides a gradual increase from simpler to more advanced exercises. This progression allows the body to gradually adapt to the demands of strength, control, and coordination of movements. It is important to build a solid foundation through propaedeutics before moving on to more advanced exercises, otherwise you risk injury or performing the exercises inefficiently.
In summary, calisthenics propaedeutics is essential for acquiring the skills needed to perform advanced exercises correctly and safely. Performing propaedeutics regularly helps improve technique, develop core strength, improve mobility, balance, and coordination, and facilitates a smooth transition to more challenging exercises.

Let's take a closer look at how these goals help prevent injuries and correct imbalances.
Calisthenics propaedeutics are particularly useful for preventing injuries, correcting muscle imbalances, and preparing the body for more challenging exercises. Find out how they can succeed in these tasks here:

Injury prevention:

Technique improvement: as we have seen, the emphasis of calisthenics propaedeutics is on learning the correct technique to perform the exercises. Proper technique reduces the risk of injury by paying attention to body alignment, weight distribution, and movement control.

Strengthening stabilizing muscles: this often involves exercises to strengthen the stabilizing muscles, which are responsible for maintaining balance and correct posture while performing exercises. Strong stabilizing muscles help avoid injury due to muscle imbalance or unwanted compensation.

Improved flexibility and mobility: propaedeutic includes joint flexibility and stretching exercises that improve muscle flexibility and joint mobility. Excellent range of motion reduces the risk of muscle or joint injury when performing calisthenics exercises.

Correction of muscle imbalances:

Targeted work on muscle groups: calisthenics exercises can be designed to focus on muscle groups that are often neglected or underdeveloped. For example, if an imbalance between upper and lower limb strength is detected, specific exercises can be performed to strengthen the weaker area and restore balance.

Strengthening neglected muscles: propaedeutics can often emphasize neglected or underdeveloped muscle groups such as trunk muscles, shoulder stabilizing muscles, or gluteal muscles. This helps correct muscle imbalances and improve symmetry and overall muscle function.

Preparation for more challenging exercises:

Building a solid foundation: propaedeutics offer a step-by-step progression to build a solid foundation of strength, control, and technology. This foundation prepares the body to tackle more challenging exercises safely and effectively.

Basic Skills Development: Calisthenics propaedeutics are used to improve basic strength, coordination, balance, and flexibility. These basic skills are essential for maintaining body weight and performing more advanced calisthenics exercises such as pull-ups, push-ups, or human flags.

Let us review some traditional propaedeutics:

Propaedeutics for pull-ups: before venturing into full pull-ups, it makes sense to start with supported or negative pull-up exercises, using a chair or lower bar to reduce body weight. In this way, you will gradually develop the strength needed for full pull-ups.

Propaedeutics for push-ups: in push-ups, you can perform simpler variations such as push-ups with support on the knees or push-ups with handstand on a raised handle. These exercises help build the strength needed for the chest, shoulder, and triceps for traditional push-ups.

Propaedeutics for lunges: supported lunges are a great way to start. With the help of a chair or bench, you can reduce body weight and gradually approach full lunges. In addition, static lunges, which maintain a bent knee position for a few seconds, are useful for improving leg stability and strength.

Abdominal exercises: to strengthen the abdominal muscles, you can perform exercises such as Cat Lunges, Reverse Crunches or Floor Crunches. With these exercises you can stabilize the trunk and prepare it for more advanced exercises such as V-Sit Crunches or Dragon Flags.

Propaedeutics for the split: before attempting a full split, you can perform exercises to improve leg mobility, such as long lunges. Gradual improvement of hip and leg mobility is essential for the correct and safe performance of the split.

Preparation for the human flag: the human flag requires strong abdominal and shoulder strength. In preparation, exercises such as lateral planks, trunk twists and lateral lunges can be performed to improve lateral body stability.

Propaedeutics for planks: planks require a high level of shoulder and trunk strength. Before venturing into a full plank, you can perform exercises such as advanced, incline or supported planks with the help of a bench or parallel bars.

Calisthenics propaedeutics are essential for developing a solid foundation of strength, agility, and body control. Be sure to incorporate them into your training program to better prepare you for more advanced exercises. Always remember to perform the exercises correctly and listen to your body's signals to avoid injury.

Frequency and duration of propaedeutic sessions

The frequency and duration of calisthenics propaedeutic sessions can vary depending on your needs, your current fitness level, and the goals you wish to achieve. Below are some points to consider when planning the frequency and duration of propaedeutic sessions.

Frequency of sessions:

For beginners: If you are new, you can start with 2-3 sessions a week, devoted exclusively to propaedeutics. Then you have enough time to learn the exercises and perform them correctly without overloading your body.
For experts and professionals: once you have mastered the basic technique, you can increase the frequency of sessions to 3-4 times a week or even more if your body is sufficiently rested and ready for training. However, remember to balance frequency with recovery, as the training propensity and exertion can be exhausting to the muscular and nervous systems.

Duration of sessions:

The duration of a calisthenics propaedeutics session can vary from 15 to 45 minutes depending on the complexity of the exercises, the number of exercises to be performed, and the rest time between sets. Start with shorter units, especially if you are a beginner, and gradually increase the duration as you gain strength and endurance.

Make sure you have enough time to do the preparatory exercises correctly and focus on proper technique and movement control. Avoid rushing just to cover a certain number of exercises in a certain amount of time. It is better to exercise for a shorter period of time with the right quality in execution than to perform several exercises incorrectly.
If you are short on time, you can focus on the preparatory exercises most important to your goals or focus on a certain area of the body in each session.
It is important to note that the frequency and duration of training sessions can be subjective and depend on your individual abilities, recovery time, and the goals you want to achieve. The most important thing is to find a balance between work and rest so that your body has time to adapt and recover from training.

If you still have doubts or uncertainties, here are some tips for planning training sessions that include propaedeutic calisthenics:

Start with a general warm-up workout: before you start with Calisthenics, you should do a short general warm-up workout to raise your body temperature and prepare your muscles for the workout. You can easily jog for a few minutes, jump rope, or do dynamic warm-up exercises such as arm and leg movements.
Take as much time as you need for calisthenics propaedeutics during your training session. Then, you can focus on performing the exercises correctly and get the maximum benefit.
Organize your propaedeutic training according to your goals: if you pursue specific goals, such as improving joint mobility or developing trunk strength, you should align your propaedeutic exercises with these goals. For example, if you want to improve shoulder mobility, you can start with shoulder mobilization exercises, such as rotations with sticks or elastic bands.
Alternate between different muscle groups: to avoid overexertion of a particular muscle group, alternate between different muscle groups during the propaedeutic phase. For example, you can start with shoulder mobility exercises, then move to core exercises and finally perform lower limb exercises.

Gradual increases: choose propaedeutic exercises that match your current fitness level and gradually increase your level of difficulty. This way you can build a solid foundation and prevent injuries.

Appropriate breaks: make sure you take the right number of breaks between sets of preparatory exercises. Then you can recover and get ready for the next workout.

Coordination with main exercises: try to coordinate propaedeutic exercises with the main exercises in your workout. For example, if your main goal is pull-ups, you can start with propaedeutic exercises for grip strength and back muscles before moving on to the actual pull-ups.

Monitor your progress: track your progress in Calisthenics. Record time under tension, number of repetitions, or other relevant metrics to assess your progress over time. This way you can tailor your training to your results.

Propaedeutic Plan

Here you will find a possible training program with propaedeutic calisthenics that will help you develop the strength and endurance you need to perform the advanced exercises. Remember that it is important to tailor the program to your personal abilities and progress. Before starting a training program, you should always seek advice from a fitness professional who will evaluate you personally.

Day 1: free body workout

Warm-up: 10-15 minutes of light resistance training (running, jumping rope, etc.), followed by joint mobility exercises.

Squats: 3-4 sets of 8-10 repetitions. You can start with the classic squat, maintaining good technique and depth, and gradually increase the intensity by performing more advanced variations such as the pistol squat (one-legged squat).

Push-ups: 3-4 sets with 8-10 repetitions. Start with classic push-ups, where you take the correct posture and control your movements. As your strength increases, you can gradually move to more advanced variations such as diamond push-ups or one-arm push-ups.

Bar pull-ups: 3-4 sets with 8-10 repetitions. If you are not yet able to do full pull-ups, you can use a rubber band or chair to support the movement and gradually remove it.

Lunges: 3-4 sets with 8-10 repetitions per leg. Start with classic lunges and move to more advanced variations with increasing strength, such as lunges with 3-second static stop or jump lunges.

Planks: 3 sets for 30-60 seconds. Pay attention to correct posture and activate all the stabilizing muscles of the trunk during the exercise.

Day 2: Tool-assisted training

Warm-up: 10-15 minutes of light resistance training followed by joint mobility exercises.

Explosive squat: from a standing position perform 10 repetitions of explosive squat with jump.

Plank: 1 minute for 3 sets

Chair dips: 3-4 sets with 8-10 repetitions. Use a chair or parallel bars to perform dips focusing on activating the triceps and pectoral muscles.

Pull-ups on the bar: 3-4 sets with 8-10 repetitions. Use a horizontal bar or elastic bands to perform pull-ups and train back and arm traction.

Push-ups on parallel bars: 3-4 sets with 8-10 repetitions. Perform push-ups on parallel bars to allow more range of motion and stress more stabilizing muscles.

Assisted flags: 3-4 sets with 8-10 repetitions. Use a horizontal bar or stand to perform assisted dragon flags, thus training abdominal strength.

This is just an example of a training program with propaedeutic calisthenics. Remember to customize the program according to your personal abilities and progress. Also pay attention to proper nutrition, sufficient rest periods, and listen to your body during training, have fun while training!

The Future of the Calisthenic Technique

Calisthenics is in great growth and development, and the future of the sport looks very promising. One of the most obvious trends is the rise of the Calisthenics community, which is attracting more and more people around the world. Through social media, online forums, and video platforms, calisthenics enthusiasts can share their experiences, training, progress, and advice. This exchange of knowledge and support is critical to the development of the discipline as it provides an opportunity to learn, be inspired, and develop new techniques from other athletes.

One example of how social media has influenced the calisthenics community is the use of Instagram. This platform has become a hub for many calisthenics athletes who share videos of advanced exercises, instruction, and motivation. Virtual sharing has a real impact on the community and leads more and more people to try Calisthenics and join local training groups.

In addition to community growth, another trend we can see in the future of calisthenics is the use of technology. Mobile apps and handheld devices can help athletes monitor and manage their workouts, record progress, and receive feedback on training technique. These tools can be useful when it comes to setting specific goals, following personalized training programs, and measuring results over time. For example, an app can provide detailed instructions on how to properly perform an exercise, tips on posture and body alignment, and track the number of repetitions and sets completed.

Calisthenics competitions are becoming increasingly popular around the world and are another important trend in the future of this discipline. These competitions test the strength, agility, and creativity of athletes as they compete in spectacular movements and unique choreography. Calisthenics competitions can be classified into different categories, such as freestyle, static, and dynamic, and are judged by expert judges who evaluate movements according to predetermined criteria. These competitions offer athletes an opportunity to showcase their skills, inspire others, and ignite their passion for calisthenics.

There may also be advances in calisthenics-specific devices in the future. Frames, parallel bars, rings, and elastic bands are among the most common equipment in the sport, but new versions of these devices could be developed that offer more options for adjustment, stability, and safety. For example, bars with different height settings could be developed to suit certain exercises or elastic bands with variable resistance for better control of load level.

Another important consideration for the future of calisthenics concerns integration with other fitness disciplines. Calisthenics could continue to merge with other disciplines such as parkour, freestyle acrobatics, or street dance. This integration makes it possible to create new forms of training that combine strength, agility, and elegance of movement. For example, acrobatics can enrich calisthenics with aerial and acrobatic movements, while parkour can add elements such as agility and fluid movement. This synergy with other disciplines opens up new opportunities for artistic and creative expression in calisthenics.

Finally, with the growing interest in Calisthenics, scientific research on this discipline may also become more important. Scientific studies can help better understand the physiological effects of calisthenics training on the human body and find ways to optimize training and avoid injury. For example, the effectiveness of various calisthenics training protocols could be studied to improve strength, muscular endurance, or flexibility. These scientific studies can provide a solid foundation for training practices and help athletes reach their full potential.

In summary, the future of Calisthenics looks bright, with a growing community, use of technology, exciting competitions, development of special devices, integration with other disciplines, and enhanced scientific research. These developments will help make calisthenics even more accessible, interesting, and effective for people of all fitness levels and goals. And what do you think? It's time to get started!

Sports Nutrition for Calisthenics

The basic concepts of sports nutrition must be applied from the very beginning, so we will now examine the basics of nutrition in the context of calisthenics.

Sports nutrition is an essential aspect of optimal performance in calisthenics. Understanding basic nutrition concepts can support training, promote muscle recovery, and optimize results.

The concept of energy balance: energy balance refers to the balance between calories taken in through diet and calories burned through physical activity. In calisthenics, it is important to consume enough calories to meet the energy requirements of the workout. If the goal is weight loss, it may be necessary to create a controlled caloric deficit. If the goal is to build muscle mass, you may need to create a controlled caloric surplus. It is important to determine your individual caloric needs based on your weight, metabolism, and activity level.

When we are talking about macronutrients, we are describing carbohydrates, proteins and fats that form the basis of the diet. It is important to have a balance of these nutrients to support the various needs of calisthenics. Protein is critical for muscle repair and growth, carbohydrates provide energy during exercise, and fats are involved in many biological processes. Determining the appropriate ratio of macronutrients depends on various factors, such as goals, activity level, and individual tolerance threshold.

Importance of protein: Protein is particularly important in calisthenics as it promotes muscle protein synthesis and recovery. Adequate intake of high-quality protein from sources such as lean meat, fish, dairy, eggs, legumes, and plant proteins can help build and maintain muscle mass.

Carbohydrates as a source of energy: carbohydrates are the main source of energy during calisthenic training. Be sure to include complex carbohydrates such as whole grains, fruits, vegetables, and legumes in your daily diet to provide long-lasting energy and sustain your performance.

The role of fats: fats perform many important functions in the body and are essential for overall health. Choosing sources of healthy fats such as olive oil, avocados, nuts, seeds, and oily fish can contribute to a balanced diet and support cardiometabolic health.

Importance of hydration: adequate hydration is critical for optimal performance in calisthenics. Be sure to drink enough during exercise to maintain adequate water balance in your body.

Diet suited to you: each person has different nutritional needs depending on factors such as age, gender, body composition, activity level, and goals. It is important to tailor your diet to your specific needs. Consider working with a nutritionist or dietitian to create a diet plan that is right for you.
Remember that these are just some of the basic concepts of sports nutrition as it relates to calisthenics. It is important to inform yourself and experiment to find the nutritional approach that best suits you and your specific goals in calisthenics.

Calories and energy balance in calisthenics

In calisthenics, calories management and energy balance are critical to achieving desired results. Understanding the concept of energy balance will help you achieve your goals, whether you want to lose weight, gain muscle mass, or simply keep your body weight stable.

To better understand energy balance, it is necessary to consider two aspects: caloric intake and caloric expenditure.

1. Caloric intake refers to calories taken in through food and drink. It is important to know one's individual caloric needs, which depend on factors such as age, weight, height, activity level, and specific goals. Calories are needed to fuel the body during exercise and to support vital biological processes. It is important to make sure that you are getting enough calories to meet the body's energy needs and to support physical activity.

2. Caloric consumption refers to calories burned through physical activity and basal metabolic rate. Calisthenics involves intense exercise and the use of multiple muscle groups, resulting in higher caloric consumption than normal daily activities. The number of calories burned depends on the duration, intensity, and frequency of the workout. In addition, basal metabolic rate, that is, resting energy expenditure, contributes to total caloric expenditure.

To achieve your goals in calisthenics exercise, you need to create a proper energy balance. If the goal is weight loss, you need to create a caloric deficit by eating fewer calories than you burn. This can be achieved by combining a balanced diet and regular exercise. If, on the other hand, the goal is to build muscle mass, you need to create a caloric surplus by eating more calories than you burn. This will give the body the energy it needs for protein synthesis and muscle growth.

It is important to remember that energy balance must be controlled to avoid drastic changes in body weight or metabolism. Excessive caloric deficit can lead to loss of muscle mass and decreased performance, while excess calories can lead to increased body fat.

Several strategies can be used to manage energy levels during calisthenics, such as tracking calories consumed and burned, planning meals according to caloric needs, and portion control. In addition, it is important to ensure a balanced diet that contains all essential nutrients for exercise and muscle recovery.

Finally, you should consult with a nutritionist or dietitian who specializes in sports to receive advice tailored to your specific calisthenics needs. This will help you optimize your diet to maximize your results and improve your performance in calisthenics.

Macronutrients and their importance for Calisthenics

Macronutrients are the basic nutrients our bodies need to provide energy and support vital functions. In the context of calisthenics, macronutrients are important to support performance, promote muscle repair and growth, and optimize body composition. The most important macronutrients are protein, carbohydrates, and fat.

Protein: Protein is essential for muscle recovery and growth. It plays a key role in protein synthesis, the process by which the body builds and repairs muscle tissue. Common protein sources include lean meat, chicken, fish, eggs, dairy products, legumes, and plant-based products such as tofu and seitan. It is recommended that high-quality protein should be consumed at every meal to ensure adequate daily protein intake.

Carbohydrates: carbohydrates are the body's main source of energy during exercise. They provide glucose to the muscles, which is converted into usable energy. When following a calisthenic diet, it is important to choose complex whole-grain carbohydrates, such as whole grains, brown rice, quinoa, sweet potatoes, legumes, and fruits. These carbohydrates provide a sustainable source of energy and help keep blood sugar levels stable.

Fats: fats are a concentrated source of energy and play an important role in hormone production, absorption of fat-soluble vitamins, and organ protection. It is important to distinguish between saturated, unsaturated, and trans fats. Healthy fats such as avocados, nuts, seeds, olive oil and fatty fish such as salmon and mackerel are recommended. Avoid foods high in saturated and trans fats, such as fried foods and industrially processed snacks.

Fluid intake: Water is essential to maintain good fluid balance during calisthenic training. During exercise, the body loses fluids through sweating and evaporation. Drinking regularly during exercise and maintaining adequate fluid intake throughout the day is important to promote performance, muscle repair, and overall body function. Appropriate macronutrient intake will vary depending on individual needs, such as activity level, metabolism, and specific goals. It is advisable to consult with a nutritionist or dietitian to create a nutrition plan tailored to your specific calisthenics-related needs.

Balancing macronutrients and making conscious food choices will help maximize training results and improve performance in calisthenics.

The importance of protein for muscle building

Proteins play a key role in supporting muscles in calisthenics. They are made up of amino acids, the basic building blocks for building and repairing muscle tissue. Proteins are essential for protein synthesis, a process by which the body creates new muscle proteins.

During calisthenic training, muscles undergo stress and microinjuries. Adequate protein intake helps repair and rebuild damaged muscle tissue. This allows muscles to adapt and become stronger and more resilient over time.

Protein also provides a longer lasting sense of satiety than carbohydrates or fat, helping to curb appetite and maintain a balanced body composition.

For calisthenics athletes, protein intake is especially important to optimize performance and promote muscle growth. The protein sources provide a combination of essential and nonessential amino acids necessary for the protein synthesis process.

Recommended protein intake varies according to individual needs, based on factors such as body weight, physical activity, and specific goals. In general, a daily protein intake of 1.2 to 2 grams per kilogram of body weight can be considered sufficient for calisthenics athletes. However, it should be noted that protein requirements may vary, and a customized diet plan may be needed based on one's specific needs.

It is important to distribute protein intake evenly throughout the day and consume a serving of protein at each meal. This allows the body to have a constant supply of amino acids for protein synthesis. In addition, consuming a serving of protein within an hour of exercise can promote muscle recovery and protein synthesis.

Remember that protein intake alone does not guarantee muscle growth. It is necessary to combine an adequate protein diet with proper training, rest, and recovery. Maintaining a balance of other macronutrients, such as carbohydrates and fats, is equally important to support energy and vital body functions.

As we have seen, protein plays a key role in supporting muscles during calisthenic training. Eating an adequate amount of high-quality protein from a variety of sources can promote muscle recovery, repair, and growth. However, it is also important to consider other aspects of diet and training for optimal results in calisthenics. A consultation with a nutrition expert or dietitian can provide guidance tailored to your specific needs.

Carbohydrates: a source of energy for exercise

Carbohydrates are a primary source of energy for calisthenics and play a key role in athletic performance. During exercise, the body uses carbohydrates as fuel to maintain intense and prolonged muscle activity.

When carbohydrates are ingested, they are broken down into simple sugars, mainly glucose, which is absorbed into the bloodstream. The glucose is then transported to muscle cells where it is converted into usable energy through the process of glycolysis. In calisthenic training, carbohydrates provide instant energy for dynamic movements such as squats, pull-ups, and lunges, as well as for strength and endurance exercises.

A diet rich in carbohydrates can improve performance in calisthenics and lead to increased endurance, strength, and muscle power. However, it is important to choose carbohydrates wisely. Choosing complex, fiber-rich carbohydrates can provide a sustainable source of energy for a longer period of time, avoiding glycemic spikes and sudden drops.

It is important to consider the timing of carbohydrate intake to maximize the benefits of calisthenics. Before exercise, consumption of high-glycemic-index carbohydrates, such as fruits or whole grains, can provide immediate energy for exercise. During exercise, consumption of carbohydrate-containing sports drinks can help maintain energy and fluid balance.

After training, it is important to replenish depleted muscle glycogen stores by consuming carbohydrates. This contributes to muscle recovery and regeneration of energy reserves for the next workout. Choosing complex carbohydrates and high-quality protein in the post-workout meal can promote recovery and protein synthesis.

However, it is important to determine the right amount of carbohydrates to consume based on your activity level, specific goals, and individual needs. A dietitian or nutritionist can help you establish an appropriate eating plan that includes the right amount and type of carbohydrates.

In summary, carbohydrates play a key role in providing energy for calisthenics. An adequate diet of complex carbohydrates can support athletic performance, improve endurance, and facilitate muscle recovery. However, it is important to choose wisely and tailor carbohydrate intake to individual needs.

Fats: appropriate quality and quantity

Fats are another essential nutrient for practicing calisthenics, but it is important to choose them wisely and know the right quality and quantity.

Fats provide energy to the body, protect organs, promote the absorption of fat-soluble vitamins, and play an important role in hormone production. However, not all fats are equal. It is important to distinguish between saturated fats, unsaturated fats, and trans fats.

Saturated fats, which are mainly found in foods of animal origin such as meat, cheese, and dairy products, can increase the risk of cardiovascular disease if consumed in excess. It is therefore advisable to limit consumption of saturated fats and try to replace them with healthier sources of fat.

Unsaturated fats, on the other hand, are considered healthy fats and can be included in a balanced diet. They are found in foods such as fish, avocados, olives, flaxseeds, and nuts. Unsaturated fats, both monounsaturated and polyunsaturated, can help reduce the risk of cardiovascular disease, improve heart health, and control inflammation in the body.

Trans fats, on the other hand, are artificial fats produced through an industrial hydrogenation process. These fats are found in many processed foods, such as packaged snacks, margarine, and fried foods. Trans fats can increase the risk of cardiovascular disease and should therefore be avoided as much as possible.

Regarding the amount of fat to consume during physical activity, it is important to consider individual needs and specific goals. Fats are highly caloric nutrients, so it is important to limit their intake to maintain an adequate energy balance. In general, the recommended range for dietary fat intake is between 20 percent and 35 percent of total daily calories.

It is important to choose high-quality sources of fats and include them in a balanced way in the diet. Choosing healthy vegetable oils such as olive oil, coconut oil, and flaxseed oil, consuming fatty fish such as salmon and mackerel, and vegetable fat sources such as avocados, nuts, and seeds can provide a good variety of healthy fats that promote energy, health, and performance in calisthenics.

In summary, fats play an important role in calisthenics, but it is important to make a conscious choice and favor high-quality fats, such as unsaturated fats. Limiting consumption of saturated and trans fats is critical to maintaining cardiovascular health. Balancing the amount of fat consumed with energy needs and training goals is critical to support the body and performance in calisthenics.

Micronutrients for Calisthenics

As with any other physical activity, it is important to pay attention to micronutrients in calisthenics to ensure good health and overall performance. Below we will look at some of them and their role in relation to calisthenics.

Vitamins and minerals are essential for proper functioning of the body and promote physical performance. Key nutrients include vitamin D, vitamin C, vitamin E, vitamin B, calcium, magnesium, iron, and zinc. A varied and balanced diet that includes fruits, vegetables, whole grains, lean protein, and dairy products can help meet the need for these nutrients.

Vitamin D is important for bone and muscle health, promotes calcium absorption, and contributes to muscle strength. A vitamin D deficiency can affect athletic performance and increase the risk of injury. Calisthenic exercises such as pull-ups and squats require good muscle strength, which can be positively affected by vitamin D. Be sure to spend time outdoors to stimulate your body's production of vitamin D or consider supplementation if you are deficient.

Calcium is important for healthy bones and teeth. In calisthenics, good bone density is important for stability and overall strength during exercise. Some examples of calcium-rich foods are milk, yogurt, cheese, oily fish, and sesame seeds.

Iron participates in the formation of hemoglobin, which transports oxygen to muscles during exercise. An iron deficiency can lead to reduced aerobic capacity and increased muscle fatigue. In weight training, exercises such as muscle-ups and pistol squats require endurance, and adequate iron intake can aid performance. Sources of iron include meat, fish, legumes, nuts, and green leafy vegetables.

Magnesium is involved in more than 300 enzymatic reactions in the body, including energy and muscle contraction processes. A magnesium deficiency can have a negative impact on muscle performance and nerve function. In calisthenics, exercises such as push-ups and muscle raises require well-functioning muscle contraction. Magnesium-rich foods include nuts, seeds, legumes, whole grains, and green leafy vegetables.

Sufficient hydration is critical for overall well-being and to support training. In calisthenics, it is important to drink enough to maintain good performance and avoid dehydration. Water is the best choice, but other fluids such as sports drinks or diluted juices can be added.

Antioxidants, such as vitamins C and E, are important to protect the body from free radical damage caused by intense exercise. These nutrients can be obtained through a diet rich in fruits, vegetables, nuts, and seeds.

Vitamin C is a powerful antioxidant that plays a key role in muscle tissue repair and collagen production, which is important for joint health. In calisthenics, exercises such as arm push-ups and planks can stress the joints. Adequate intake of vitamin C from foods such as citrus fruits, kiwis, strawberries, and broccoli can contribute to joint health and muscle recovery.

It is important to note that nutritional intake may vary depending on individual needs, training goals, and other personal factors.

Nutrition before training for calisthenics

Pre-workout nutrition plays a key role in calisthenics, as it provides energy, improves performance, and promotes muscle recovery. It is important to take the right nutrients before training to maximize results and optimize performance. Below are some tips for nutrition before calisthenics training.

Complex carbohydrates: carbohydrates are an important source of energy for physical activity. Choose complex carbohydrates such as whole grains, whole wheat pasta, brown rice, and sweet potatoes. These foods provide long-lasting energy and help maintain optimal levels of muscle glycogen during exercise.

Lean protein: protein is important for muscle synthesis and recovery. Choose lean protein sources such as chicken, turkey, fish, eggs, or low-fat dairy products. Protein helps maintain muscle mass and promotes recovery and rebuilding of muscle tissue after exercise.

Healthy fats: including a small amount of healthy fats in your pre-workout diet can provide energy and improve absorption of some vitamins. Choose sources of healthy fats such as avocados, nuts, seeds, or vegetable oils.

Fiber: Fiber can help keep blood sugar levels stable and create a feeling of satiety. However, avoid fiber-rich foods before physical activity because they can cause gastrointestinal upset during exercise. Choose low-fiber foods, such as low-fiber cereals or fruits.

Hydration: adequate hydration before exercise is important to maintain performance and avoid dehydration. Drink plenty of water before exercise to ensure adequate hydration.

Meal schedule: It is advisable to eat a meal at least 1-2 hours before training to allow for proper digestion. This time period may vary depending on individual sensitivities. If you prefer a lighter meal or snack before your workout, you may opt for foods that are easier to digest.

Individual adaptation: the best pre-workout diet may vary according to individual preferences and specific needs. What is good for one person may be counterproductive for another. It is important to experiment and find the pre-workout dietary approach that best suits your body and needs.

Remember that pre-workout nutrition is an important aspect, but only one part of the overall equation for achieving results. You should consult a dietitian or nutritionist for advice tailored to your specific needs.

Nutrition during calisthenic training

Nutrition can help support energy, performance, and muscle recovery during intense training sessions. Calisthenics training can be very demanding, and food intake during training requires attention to avoid digestive problems. Below are some tips for nutrition during calisthenics training:

Hydration: adequate hydration during exercise is essential to maintain a good performance. Drink water regularly during exercise to avoid dehydration. For very intense or prolonged workouts, you may also consider electrolyte supplements to restore minerals lost through sweat.

Light snacks: if the workout is longer or spread over several sessions, light snacks can be eaten during breaks. Choose easily digestible, carbohydrate-rich foods, such as a banana, an energy bar, or a small portion of dried fruit. These foods provide quick energy and can help keep blood sugar levels stable during exercise.

Sports drinks: if training is particularly intense and long, choose sports drinks with carbohydrates and electrolytes to provide energy and hydration. Be sure to choose sports drinks with natural ingredients and without excessive added sugars.

Energy gels: energy gels are a convenient form of nutrition during exercise, especially during longer sessions or when solid food cannot be consumed. These gels are rich in carbohydrates and provide a quick supply of energy. Be sure to choose high-quality energy gels with natural ingredients.

Individual experimentation: Everyone reacts differently to food during exercise. It is important to experiment with different foods and strategies to find out what works best for your body. Consider your preferences, energy requirements, and feelings during exercise to determine the most appropriate nutritional approach.

Remember that nutrition during calisthenic training should be tailored to your needs and preferences.

Nutrition after training: muscle recovery and restoration

Post-exercise nutrition is critical for muscle recovery and tissue repair after intense training. During training, muscles are exposed to stresses and micro-injuries that require adequate nutrients to heal and adapt. Below are some tips for proper nutrition after calisthenics training:

Protein is essential for muscle protein repair and synthesis. Consume a high-quality protein source after training, such as lean meat, chicken, fish, eggs, dairy products, or plant-based alternatives such as legumes, tofu, or seitan. You should aim for a protein intake of about 20 to 30 grams per meal.

Carbohydrates are important to replenish muscle glycogen stores used during exercise. Consume complex carbohydrates such as whole grains, sweet potatoes, brown rice, or quinoa to provide energy and promote recovery. It is advisable to consume an adequate portion of carbohydrates along with protein after exercise.

Fruits and vegetables: generous portions of fruits and vegetables are important in the post-workout diet to provide antioxidants, vitamins, and minerals essential for recovery and overall health. Choose berries, citrus fruits, green leafy vegetables, and other colorful varieties to maximize nutrient intake.

Don't forget to include sources of healthy fats in your post-workout diet. Omega-3 essential fatty acids found in foods such as oily fish, flaxseeds, chia seeds and walnuts can reduce inflammation and promote muscle recovery.

Hydration: drinking enough water after exercise is important to keep the body hydrated and aid the recovery process. It is advisable to drink water throughout the day and increase water intake after exercise, especially if you have been sweating a lot.

Timing: it is advisable to eat a protein and carbohydrate meal or snack within 1 to 2 hours of training to maximize muscle recovery. This time interval is known as the "anabolic window," when the body is particularly receptive to nutrients for protein synthesis and muscle recovery.

Each person may respond differently to post-workout nutrition. It is important to experiment and observe how the body responds to different foods and strategies. For example, some people benefit from a solid meal immediately after exercise, while others prefer a protein shake or a light snack. Listen to your body and adapt your diet to your needs and preferences.

Remember that post-workout nutrition is only part of the big picture. An overall balanced diet and good meal planning based on your goals are critical for optimal performance and long-term muscle recovery. A consultation with a dietitian or nutritionist can provide guidance tailored to your needs.

The importance of hydration in calisthenics

Hydration is extremely important in calisthenics and any other form of exercise. Water performs several important functions in the human body, and proper hydration can have a significant impact on physical performance, recovery, and overall health. The importance of hydration in calisthenics is explained below:

Body temperature regulation: during intense physical activity, the body produces heat, which can lead to an increase in body temperature. Water helps regulate body temperature through the process of sweating and evaporation of sweat on the skin. Proper hydration allows the body to maintain optimal core temperature for optimal physical performance and avoid overheating.

Nutrient supply: Water plays a key role in transporting nutrients to muscle cells. Good hydration allows for good blood circulation and ensures that important nutrients such as carbohydrates, proteins, and minerals reach the muscles efficiently. This promotes muscle recovery, protein synthesis, and tissue regeneration.

Supports metabolic functions: Water is involved in numerous metabolic processes in the body, including digestion, absorption of nutrients, and elimination of metabolic waste products. Good hydration helps maintain normal functioning of internal organs and supports efficient metabolism.

Joint lubrication: calisthenics involves complex joint movements that require good mobility and flexibility. Water helps lubricate joints, reducing the risk of injury, friction, and joint pain during exercise.

Prevention of fatigue and fatigue: Dehydration can lead to reduced physical performance, endurance, and muscle strength. Drinking enough during exercise helps prevent premature fatigue and allows for greater endurance and improved athletic performance.

Muscle recovery and tissue repair: after exercise, adequate hydration is essential for the process of muscle recovery and repair of damaged tissues. Water provides the necessary environment for the transport of nutrients to muscle cells and for the elimination of toxins and waste products of metabolism.

Support electrolyte balance: during exercise, the body loses fluids and important electrolytes such as sodium, potassium, and magnesium through sweat. Sufficient water intake helps maintain the body's electrolyte balance and ensure proper functioning of muscle and nerve cells.

To ensure adequate hydration during regular exercise, it is advisable to drink water before, during and after exercise. The amount of fluid needed depends on the intensity of physical activity, environmental temperature, age, and individual condition. It is important to listen to one's body and drink according to thirst, as well as observe the color of urine as a general indicator of hydration status. In addition, during prolonged or intense exercise, you can supplement hydration with sports drinks containing electrolytes to restore the balance of minerals lost through sweating.

In summary, adequate hydration in calisthenics is critical for physical performance, muscle recovery, and overall health. Drinking enough before, during, and after exercise helps keep the body hydrated, improve endurance, and avoid the risk of dehydration and its negative consequences.

Is supplementation useful in calisthenics?

Supplements are attractive to many calisthenics athletes who want to maximize performance, promote muscle recovery, and support overall health. However, it is important to consider some factors before starting a supplement. The following are some points to consider:

Personal goals: Before deciding to take a supplement, you should review your goals in calisthenics. If your goal is to increase muscle mass, improve endurance or strength, you should consider supplementing with specific nutrients or substances that support these goals.

Balanced diet: dietary supplements should never replace a balanced and varied diet. Before considering supplements, make sure you are eating well and getting all the essential nutrients your body needs. Focus on eating whole foods rich in vitamins, minerals, and antioxidants.

Pro tip: Before you start supplementing your diet, it is a good idea to consult a physician, such as a nutritionist or a physician specializing in sports nutrition. This way you can determine whether you really need to supplement your diet and which nutrients or supplements may be suitable for your specific needs.

Targeted supplementation: depending on your goals and needs, you may consider taking certain supplements. For example, if you want to increase muscle mass, you may choose protein supplements such as whey protein powder or other protein-containing foods. If you need muscle recovery support, you might consider taking supplements containing branched-chain amino acids (BCAAs) or glutamine.

Product quality: when choosing dietary supplements, be sure to select high-quality products from reputable brands. Pay attention to ingredient content and manufacturing standards. Read product labels carefully and check for safety and purity.

Side effects and contraindications: It is important to know that taking supplements may be associated with side effects and contraindications. Some supplements may interact with medications or pre-existing conditions. Be sure to be aware of any risks and always consult a physician before beginning any form of supplementation.

In summary, supplementation in calisthenics can be considered to support training goals and overall health, but it is important to consider the factors mentioned above. Consultation with a health professional and a balanced diet should always come first. Taking supplements should be an addition to the diet and not a substitute for good nutrition and a healthy lifestyle.

Food plans and dietary strategies for Calisthenics

Nutritional plans and strategies for calisthenics can vary depending on individual goals, activity levels, and personal preferences. However, there are some general guidelines that can be followed to optimize performance and recovery in calisthenics. The following are some important points to consider when planning your diet:

Calories and energy balance: determining the correct caloric intake is critical to achieving your goals in calisthenics. You may need a caloric surplus to gain muscle mass but a caloric deficit to lose weight. Calculate your caloric needs based on your basal metabolic rate, activity level, and specific goals.

Macronutrients: the most important macronutrients are carbohydrates, proteins, and fats. It is important to balance the intake of these nutrients according to your needs. Protein is critical for muscle repair and growth, so be sure to consume an adequate amount of high-quality protein. Carbohydrates provide energy for training and should be present in your diet in sufficient amounts. Healthy fats are important for overall health and can contribute to hormone balance.

Whole foods: provide the body with a variety of whole foods such as fruits, vegetables, whole grains, lean proteins, dairy products, legumes, and vegetable oils. These foods provide vitamins, minerals, fiber, and antioxidants that are important for overall well-being and to support muscles.

Meal distribution: organize meals to provide sufficient energy before exercise and promote recovery after exercise. The pre-workout meal should consist mainly of carbohydrates and protein to provide energy and nutrients to the muscles. The post-workout meal should contain a combination of carbohydrates and protein to promote muscle repair and recovery.

Hydration: adequate hydration is essential for calisthenics performance and recovery. Be sure to drink enough before, during, and after your workout. Water is the best choice, but electrolyte-based sports drinks can also be considered if the activity is intense and of long duration.

Adaptation: adapt the diet to your individual needs. Consider food intolerances, personal preferences, and special needs. If you have difficulty planning your diet, you can consult a nutritionist specialized in sports nutrition, who can develop a diet plan tailored to your goals and needs.

Remember that nutrition for calisthenics is an individual process, and what works for one person may not work for another. Experiment and observe how your body responds to different diets and adjust your plan accordingly.

Body weight management in calisthenics gymnastics

Body weight control is an important aspect of calisthenics, as weight directly affects the ability to perform certain exercises and increase overall performance. The following are some points to keep in mind when practicing calisthenics to control body weight:

Define goals: Before starting any weight management program, define your goals. You may lose weight, gain muscle mass, or maintain a healthy, balanced body weight. This will help you determine your strategies and tactics.

Balanced diet: a balanced and appropriate diet is critical to controlling body weight in calisthenics. Be sure to eat a variety of nutritious foods such as fruits, vegetables, lean proteins, whole grains, and healthy fats. Avoid processed and sugary foods and those high in saturated fats.

Portion control: portion control is important to avoid excess calories or excessive restriction. Learn to identify appropriate portion sizes to avoid eating too much or too little. Tools such as a kitchen scale or measuring cup can be used to calculate the right amount of food.

Regular physical activity: in addition to calisthenics, you should include other forms of physical activity, such as resistance and strength training, in your routine. Regular physical activity helps burn calories, increase metabolism, and improve body composition.

Monitor weight and body measurements: keep track of your weight and body measurements regularly to assess progress and make any changes to your diet and exercise program. Remember that body weight alone is not the only indicator of progress, as body composition can change even without a significant change in weight.

Patience and consistency: controlling body weight requires patience and consistency over time. Do not expect immediate results but focus on small and steady progress. Maintain a regular exercise program and be sure to follow a balanced diet to achieve the desired long-term results.

Remember that weight control in calisthenics is an individual process and it may take some time to find the right approach for you. If you are in doubt or need more detailed guidance, it is always advisable to consult a nutrition expert or an experienced calisthenics coach.

Nutrition for endurance and strength in calisthenics

Nutrition plays a key role in the development of endurance and strength in calisthenics. A balanced diet can provide the body with the nutrients it needs to sustain intense training, promote muscle growth, and improve overall performance. Below is a detailed guide to nutrition for endurance and strength in calisthenics:

Adequate calories: Be sure to consume enough calories to meet the energy requirements of training and promote muscle growth. Calorie requirements depend on age, weight, height, physical activity level, and specific goals. You can calculate your daily caloric needs using specific formulas or by seeking advice from an experienced nutritionist.

Protein is important for muscle building and recovery. Be sure to include high-quality protein sources such as lean meat, chicken, fish, eggs, dairy products, legumes, and tofu in your diet. Try to distribute your protein intake evenly throughout the day to promote muscle protein synthesis.

Carbohydrates: carbohydrates are the main source of energy for endurance and strength training. Choose complex carbohydrates such as whole grains, brown rice, whole wheat pasta, sweet potatoes, and legumes. These foods provide long-lasting energy and help strength last longer during exercise.

Fats: healthy fats are important for overall health and can provide additional energy during exercise. Choose sources of healthy fats such as avocados, nuts, seeds, vegetable oils (such as olive oil and flaxseed oil) and fatty fish. Ensure a balanced intake of fats in the diet to avoid excess calories.

Hydration: adequate hydration is critical to maintain performance during exercise and promote recovery. Drink plenty of water throughout the day and increase fluid intake during intense training sessions. Remember that fluid requirements may vary depending on environmental conditions and training intensity.

Fiber and vegetables: fiber is important for digestive health and can help you feel full. Be sure to include lots of leafy green vegetables, fruits, whole grains, and legumes in your diet to get enough fiber.

Pre-workout snack: Have a light snack with carbohydrates and protein about 1 to 2 hours before your workout. This provides sustained energy during exercise and promotes muscle protein synthesis.

Nutrition for flexibility and mobility in calisthenics

Nutrition is also important in calisthenics to improve range of motion, fluidity, and elasticity of the body. A balanced and appropriate diet can promote healthy joints, muscles, and connective tissue to improve performance and reduce the risk of injury. Below is detailed information on nutrition for flexibility and mobility in calisthenics:

Eat antioxidants: antioxidants are nutrients that fight free radicals and reduce inflammation in the body. Examples of foods rich in antioxidants are colorful fruits and vegetables such as berries, citrus fruits, spinach, kale, peppers, and carrots. Antioxidants help reduce oxidative stress, which can damage tissue and limit mobility.

Omega-3 fatty acids: Omega-3 fatty acids are known for their anti-inflammatory properties and can promote healthy joints and connective tissue. Some sources of omega-3 fatty acids include fatty fish such as salmon, mackerel and sardines, flaxseeds, chia seeds and walnuts. Inclusion of omega-3 in the diet can help maintain joint flexibility and mobility.

Collagen: Collagen is a protein that makes up much of the body's connective tissue, including tendons, ligaments, and cartilage. Consuming collagen-rich foods, such as lean meat, fish, eggs, and bone broth, can promote healthy joints and connective tissue. In addition, taking collagen supplements can help improve flexibility and mobility.

Hydration: adequate fluid intake is important to keep body tissues supple. Be sure to drink enough throughout the day, especially during physical activity. Water is the best source of fluids, but you can also consume drinks such as green tea, herbal teas or fruit and vegetable smoothies to increase your fluid intake.

Vitamins and minerals: Some vitamins and minerals are essential for healthy joints and tissues. Be sure to eat a balanced diet that includes a variety of foods rich in vitamins and minerals such as calcium, magnesium, vitamin C, vitamin D and vitamin E. These nutrients are found in foods such as dairy products, fish, fruits, green leafy vegetables, and nuts.

Anti-inflammatory foods: inflammation can limit joint flexibility and mobility. Consuming foods with anti-inflammatory properties can help reduce inflammation in the body. These are foods such as ginger, turmeric, chili peppers, garlic, onions, and olive oil. When included in the diet, these foods can help with flexibility and mobility.

It is important to remember that diet alone is not enough to improve flexibility and mobility in calisthenics. Therefore, it is essential to combine a balanced diet with an appropriate stretching and specific training program. Consultation with a nutritionist or dietitian who specializes in calisthenics can provide individualized advice to optimize nutrition according to individual needs and goals.

Printed in Great Britain
by Amazon